Leading Young Catholics into Scripture

FUN AND CREATIVE WAYS
TO BRING THE BIBLE TO LIFE

Leading Young Catholics into Scripture

FUN and **CREATIVE** Ways
to Bring the Bible to Life

Mary Kathleen Glavich, SND

TWENTY THIRD *23rd*
PUBLICATIONS

DEDICATION

This book is dedicated to the catechists of the church
who share the Good News with patience, perseverance, and love.
May this word of God be fulfilled in them:

"You will shine in the world like bright stars
because you are offering it the word of life."
PHILIPPIANS 2:15–16 JB

TWENTY-THIRD PUBLICATIONS
One Montauk Avenue, Suite 200
PO Box 6015
New London, CT 06320
(860) 437-3012
(800) 321-0411

Cover images: © iStockphoto / MasaruHorie

ISBN 978-1-58595-800-9
Library of Congress Catalog Card Number 2010925841
Printed in the U.S.A.

ACKNOWLEDGMENTS

"Israel's Greatest King" (Illustration B) is adapted from its original form in *God Calls a People* from the CHRIST OUR LIFE series written by the Sisters of Notre Dame and published by Loyola University; "The Lost Coin" (page 19) and "Abraham: A Rap" (page 119) are taken from the same series.

The modern version of Psalm 23 (page 28), the crossword puzzle (pages 125-127), and the original form of "Queen Esther" (pages 104-107) appeared in *Called by the Father*, Teacher's Manual and Resource Book written by Mary Kathleen Glavich, SND, and Mary Loretta Pastva, SND, from the *Light of the World* series published by Benziger Publishing Co.

"Jonah, Patron of Catechists" (pages 77-78) first appeared in *Catechist* magazine, September 1982, and is reprinted here by permission of the publisher, Peter Li, Inc., 2451 E. River Rd., Dayton OH 45439.

Unless otherwise noted, Scripture texts used in this work are taken from *The New American Bible*, copyright ©1970, by the Confraternity of Christian Doctrine, Washington, DC, and are used by permission of the copyright owner. All rights reserved.

Scripture texts taken from *The Jerusalem Bible*, copyright ©1966, Darton, Longman and Todd, Ltd., and Doubleday & Company, Inc., are marked as such and are used by permission of the publisher.

Special thanks to Rita Mary Harwood, SND, Melannie Svoboda, SND, Mary David Horan, SND, Mary Martha Maynard, SND, and the other sisters in my community who encouraged me to give the talk at an NCEA convention which led to this book.

I am also grateful to Regina Marie Alfonso, SND, Mary Shelia Keily, SND, Don Curran, and Millie Sussman for their assistance.

Attempts have been made to identify the sources of original material. If there has been an oversight, please inform us so that we can provide the rightful acknowledgment.

CONTENTS

Introduction

Lord, help me to lead my students into Scripture in such a way that they make the prayer of Jeremiah their own: "When I found your words, I devoured them; they became my joy and the happiness of my heart." JEREMIAH 15:16

This is a perfect prayer for catechists, for by leading our students into Scripture, we carry on the Christian mission in the spirit of Christ and the first Christians. When Jesus met the two disciples on the way to Emmaus, it was through Scripture that he taught them about himself (Luke 24:27). When Philip encountered the Ethiopian reading Isaiah, he asked, "Do you really grasp what you are reading?" The man replied, "How can I unless someone explains it to me?" Philip then proceeded to announce the Good News based on the text the man was reading. The Ethiopian was baptized and went on his way rejoicing (Acts 8:29–39). When we introduce our students to God's word and teach them its meaning, we too are apostles spreading the Good News.

WHAT IS THE BIBLE?

The Bible is the word of God in the words of human beings, "living and effective, sharper than any two-edged sword" (Hebrews 4:12). The word of God in Scripture is the same powerful word that was at work at creation. When God said, "Let there be," the whole universe exploded into being. The word in Scripture is the same as the word of Jesus, which calmed wind and waves, healed people, and brought the dead back to life. A centurion whose servant was sick knew the power of Jesus' word. He came to Jesus and pleaded, "Say but the word and my servant will be healed." At the word of Jesus, the servant was cured. The Church has no blessing for the Bible. The Bible doesn't need one because it is God's word.

We know that God broke into our lives and was revealed in the form of Jesus, whom we call the Word made flesh. God has also chosen to communicate to us through the words of Scripture. The *Catechism of the Catholic Church* points out that the Church has always venerated the Scriptures as she venerates the Lord's Body. At the Eucharist we are nourished both at the table of God's word and the table of Christ's body. Like the human word Jesus, Scripture is divine. It can be misunderstood, and its humanity or its divinity can be overstressed.

The Bible is a picture of God. A little girl was busy drawing at the kitchen table. Her mother asked, "What are you doing?" The girl answered, "I'm drawing a picture of God." The mother, smiling, responded, "But, honey, no one knows what God looks like!" Undaunted, the girl replied, "They will when I'm through!" All of us are piecing together a picture of God throughout our lives. We're trying to figure out who God is and what God is like. Scripture gives us a reliable picture of God. In fact, it is as God wants to be known.

The Bible is a sacramental. In *With Hearts Burning*, a book on the Eucharist, Henri Nouwen points out that the word of God makes present what it indicates. Merely hearing God's word can change us. Nouwen recalls the two disciples on the way to Emmaus after the crucifixion. They had lost all hope, but when a stranger, who was the risen Lord, met up with them and explained Scripture, their hearts burned. They experienced his presence. The full power of the word does not lie in how we apply it after we have heard it. The transforming power of the word does its divine work as we listen.

The Bible is a mirror that reflects ourselves and our human race, our grandeur and our folly. As we try to find ourselves and discover who we are, as we search for meaning in our lives, the Bible is at hand to reveal our identity and our ultimate destiny.

The Bible is a global positioning system through which God directs us as we journey to our promised land. "All scripture is inspired by God and can profitably be used for teaching, for refuting error, for guiding people's lives and leading them to be holy" (2 Timothy 3:16, *Jerusalem Bible*).

The Bible is a love letter in which God reassures us that we are loved and have been saved. It has been called "a book drenched in love." In the words of Scripture, God manifests a passionate love for us. God pursues us despite our imperfections, our stubbornness, our hard-heartedness. More than once in Scripture God uses the intimate bond between a husband and a wife to symbolize our relationship. Reading God's words, listening to them, reflecting on them, we come not only to know that God loves us but also to experience, to feel, God's love for us. Our relationship with God deepens.

The Bible is a springboard for prayer, for dialogue with God who speaks through it. The *Constitution on Divine Revelation* states, "In the sacred books the Father who is in heaven comes lovingly to meet his children and talks with them" (21). The Bible is God's 1-800 number. The call is free. You never get a busy signal. You're never put on hold. Best of all, you never get an answering machine saying, "Hello. This is God. I'm not in my office now." The Bible even has a 911 number. It is Luke 9:11—"He received them and spoke to them about the kingdom, and he healed those who needed to be cured." This tells how God saved us through Jesus when the human race was in a state of emergency. God saves us through the Bible in a similar way. When we read it, God receives us, speaks to us, and, yes, heals us.

Most significantly, the Bible is a good way to know Jesus, for as Cardinal John Henry Newman wrote:

> …while the thought of Christ is but a creation of our minds, it may gradually be changed or fade away, it may become defective or perverted; whereas when we contemplate Christ as manifested in the Gospels…then we shall at length believe in him with a conviction, a confidence, and an entireness, which can no more be annihilated than the belief in our senses. » *Parochial and Plain Sermons III*, p. 131

Jesus himself makes familiarity with God's word and obedience to it essential for anyone who desires a relationship with him:

> "If you make my word your home you will indeed be my disciples. You will learn the truth and the truth shall make you free." » John 8:31–32, *Jerusalem Bible*

And again, "My mother and my brothers are those who hear the word of God and put it into practice." » Luke 8:21, *Jerusalem Bible*

WHY IS IT IMPORTANT TO TEACH STUDENTS SCRIPTURE?

Students need to become familiar with the Bible so that all their lives they do not think that Jesus cured leopards instead of lepers or that an epistle is the wife of an apostle. A Gallup poll reported that basic Bible knowledge is at a record low. Half of the Christians polled did not know that Jesus preached the Sermon on the Mount. Gallup observed that Americans say they believe the Ten Commandments, but they can't name them. And some Christians who are in church on Easter don't know what they are commemorating. Gallup summed up the situation by saying, "The startling fact is Americans do not know what they believe or why....Bible illiteracy presents not only a spiritual or religious problem in this nation but a cultural one as well."

The Bible is an integral part of our culture. Knowing about the Bible is part of being educated. Much of civilization's literature, music, and art will be closed to our children if they lack a biblical background. I remember wondering at a performance of Mendelssohn's *Elijah* how many people in the audience had the knowledge to appreciate this masterpiece fully.

The Bible has even influenced our speech. Expressions such as "Can a leopard change its spots?" "the handwriting on the wall," "the blind leading the blind," "sour grapes," "the patience of Job," "as old as Methuselah," and "scapegoat" originated in Scripture.

Bible illiteracy prevents many Catholic adults from turning to Scripture for information, inspiration, or guidance. We can help our students, the next generation of adults, to read the Bible and to recognize it as God's word.

Students need to understand the real truth behind the stories of the Bible so that when they discover that many of them were not meant to be interpreted literally, they will not discard belief in God along with belief in the stories.

Young Catholics today are often helpless when they deal with persons who quote Scripture liberally to evangelize or proselytize them.

Our children thirst for an encounter with God that will give meaning and joy to their lives; that encounter can happen through Scripture.

As we pray and reflect on Scripture, we imitate Mary, our Mother, the first and best disciple of the Lord. Mary teaches us to treasure God's words and actions and to ponder them in our hearts.

HOW WILL THIS BOOK HELP?

If you are reading this page, chances are you are already convinced of the value of Scripture and the need for leading young Catholics into its riches. You are probably looking for ways to teach the Bible. This book will help you plan scriptural activities that are effective and at the same time enjoyable. It will help you add variety to your plans and forestall those words that make a teacher's heart sink: "This is boring." A Protestant group claims: "It is a sin to bore children with the Gospel." A Catholic bishop amended this slogan: "A mortal sin!"

Each of the thirty chapters in this book presents a general method to lead students into Scripture. Specific activities and examples illustrate how each method can be carried out across age levels from preschool to adult. You can use your common sense and experience in adapting the material in this book to your class, situation, and teaching style. Besides being useful in themselves, the suggestions are meant to be catalysts for your own creative ideas.

With the thirty methods described here, and through the Holy Spirit working in us, we can entice our students to taste God's word. Once their appetite is whetted, they will be more apt to turn to the Bible for daily nourishment. They might even come to devour it!

CHAPTER 1

Read the Bible

Two college freshmen who were bombarded with questions from Scripture by a fundamentalist on campus were made painfully aware of their ignorance. They asked me what they could do to know Scripture better. I recommended a book: the Bible itself! A simple way to get students to know the Bible is to have them read it. In your religion classes, opt for a textbook that is woven with Scripture and that sends the students to the Bible. If possible, have a Bible for each student. (Attractive, inexpensive Bibles are available through the American Bible Society, www.americanbible.org.)

Sharing the Light of Faith: The National Catechetical Directory recommends that older students use the Bible as a supplementary text (n. 264). Beginning readers, too, should have the joy of reading the Bible through carefully selected passages or adapted versions. The well-loved *Arch Books* for children present more than seventy Bible stories in delightful booklets. See Resources, page 90.

For younger children, when a Bible passage is used during a lesson, you might read it from the Bible or from a card with a simplified version that is inserted in your Bible. That way the children associate the passage with God's book.

The following suggestions and activities help immerse students in the Bible:

In class allow God's word to speak to your students directly. Give them time to read the Bible. Take them to church or some other quiet place and have them spread out as far away from one another as possible to read, reflect, and pray over a passage. This is not wasted time. It underlines the importance you place on Bible reading.

Explain different ways to read the Bible:

Bit-by-bit: Read only one or two lines and let them sink into you.

Book-by-book: Read an entire book. Short books like the Gospel of Mark can be read in one sitting.

Bird's eye: Skim a book reading only the section headings in boldface print and then reflect on the impact of the whole.

One track: Read according to a theme: prayer, faith, forgiveness, justice, women, trees. Use a concordance, index, or online Bible site to locate verses.

Methodical: Read the Bible straight through, beginning to end.

Liturgical: Read the readings for the day's eucharistic celebration.

Marian: Pray the rosary using mysteries from Scripture other than the traditional twenty. Read a passage before each decade and then meditate on it during that decade.

Fr. David Knight's way: Keep your Bible on your pillow. Every night read one line. Anyone can read just one line a night. What will happen is that you will get carried away and sometimes read two or three lines. Before you know it, you'll have read a book!

Lectio divina: Read and pray the Bible according to the four steps of the monastic method described on pages 57-58.

Encourage the students to write in their Bibles: annotate them, write in margins, underline, highlight, circle, and star verses.

Prepare for upcoming Scripture readings together. Use helps like *At Home with the Word*, published by Liturgy Training Publications (www.ltp.org; 1-800-933-1800). Discuss the readings. Pray over them. Let students themselves conduct these weekly preparation sessions.

Use a Lectionary-based religion series or begin a Bible study club in your school or parish.

Assign biblical passages as homework to be discussed in the next class.

Acquaint your students with the structure of the Bible and instruct them in the mechanics of finding their way around in it. Have them look at the table of contents and answer questions such as the following:

1. What are the two main divisions of the Bible?

2. What are the subdivisions?

3. Which books are named after men? After women?

4. Which books seem to contain history?

5. Which books are in pairs?

6. Which books are popular?

7. Which books have you never heard of?

8. What is the first book in the Bible? The last?

9. What is the shortest book in the Bible? The longest?

10. Which one would you like to read? Why?

Teach Scripture references by comparing them to an address.

For example:	Jeremiah	Title (City)
	17:	Chapter (Street)
	7–8	Verses (House Number)

Point out how chapters and verses are marked on the pages of the Bible. Make sure the students understand where the chapters and verses begin.

Ask questions that make use of interesting cross references and footnotes.

To familiarize your students with the abbreviations of the books, play "Travel":

First, make flashcards of some Bible abbreviations. Then direct one student to stand beside the desk of a classmate. Have the two students race to name the book that corresponds to the abbreviation shown. The winner gets to stand beside the next player's desk. See who in the class can travel the farthest.

Hold a contest in which the winner is the one who discovers the most biblical books in a word search puzzle. (See Illustration A in the Appendix.)

Have a student name a book of the Bible and call on someone to tell the books that come before and after it. The one who answers then names yet another book.

Provide practice in looking up verses and in writing Scripture references. Have students write references for verses they like and exchange them. Or carry out this creative activity:

Distribute a letter from God composed of lines from the Bible given in the form of references. In order to read the letter, the students must look up the references and write only the words of the verse that are indicated. When they are finished, they should slowly and prayerfully read what they have written.

Here is a sample "love letter from God" based on texts from the *New American Bible* and with the answers provided:

Dear _____ *,*

Isaiah 43:1 (words 24–32)	*I have called you by name: you are mine.*
Jeremiah 31:3 (words 8–14)	*With age-old love I have loved you.*
Deuteronomy 1:31 (words 13–32)	*Your God carried you, as a man carries a child, all along your journey until you arrived at this place.*
Isaiah 54:10 (words 1–17)	*Though the mountains leave their place and the hills be shaken, my love shall never leave you.*
John 15:9 (words 1–10)	*As the Father loves me, so l have loved you.*
Song of Songs 8:6 (words 1–8)	*Set me as a seal on your heart.*
Psalm 50:15 (words 1–12)	*Then call upon me in time of distress; I will rescue you.*

Love, God

Teach the children to read Scripture as they would a letter from someone very important in their lives, slowly, wringing the meaning out of every phrase, reading between the lines, and reading certain parts over and over.

Challenge the students to translate the following recipe for a Bible Cake. The answers are in parentheses.

½ lb Psalms 55:22 (butter)	2 cups Nahum 3:12 (figs)
2 cups Jeremiah 6:20 (sugar)	2 cups 1 Samuel 30:12 (raisins)
½ dozen Jeremiah 17:11 (eggs)	1 cup Numbers 17:23 (almonds)
3½ cups 1 Kings 5:2 (flour)	2 tsp 1 Samuel 14:25 (honey)
Pinch of Leviticus 2:13 (salt)	2 Chronicles 9:9 (spices: cinnamon,
2 tsp Amos 4:5 (yeast: baking powder)	ground cloves, nutmeg)
1½ cups Judges 4:19 (milk)	

Then see Proverbs 23:14. (Beat)

Bake 1–1½ hours at 350°. Makes 2 loaves. (Source Unknown)

Have the children translate the following recipe for cookies based on the *New American Bible*.

½ cup Psalms 55:22 (butter)

1 cup Jeremiah 6:20 (sugar)

1 Job 39:14 (egg)

T Judges 4:19 second sentence (milk)

1¼ cups 1 Kings 5:2 eleventh word (flour)

¼ tsp Leviticus 2:13 (salt)

¼ tsp Amos 4:5 (baking powder)

¼ tsp each of 2 Chronicles 9:9
(nutmeg, cloves, and cinnamon)

Cream items 1 and 2. Add item 3 and beat. Add item 4 and stir. Gradually add items 5, 6, 7, and 8. Mix well and set by teaspoon on buttered cookie sheet, one inch apart. Bake at 375° for about eight minutes. (Source Unknown)

Hold a contest for finding verses as described in Chapter 21, "Play Bible Games" (page 66).

Design activities for which the students look up passages to locate information. For example, to discover the seven last words of Jesus, send them to Luke 23:34; Luke 23:43; John 19:26–27; John 19:28; Mark 15:34; John 19:30; Luke 23:46.

Or to find images that John used for Jesus, give these references: John 6:35; John 8:12; John 10:7; John 10:11; John 11:25; John 15:1.

Or have them search for any general topic such as animals, birds, colors, flowers, mothers, or fathers.

These searches can be in the form of a matching exercise. For example, have the students match the seven sorrows of Mary with the verses that describe them (as below):

1. ___John 19:25–27

2. ___Luke 2:33–35

3. ___Luke 2:41–50

4. ___Luke 23:50–55

5. ___Matthew 2:13–18

6. ___Mark 15:16–22

7. ___John 19:38–42

A. The flight into Egypt

B. The prophecy of Simeon

C. Jesus lost in the Temple

D. Meeting Jesus carrying his cross

E. Mary at the foot of the cross

F. Jesus taken down from the cross

G. The burial of Jesus

(Answers: 1=E; 2=B; 3=C; 4=F; 5=A; 6=D; 7=G)

Invite students to match Scripture references with summaries of verses, or let them look up the references and summarize the verses themselves.

Give the students sets of three Scripture references for verses on the same topic. Have them look up the references and tell what they have in common. The class might work in groups of three with each student responsible for reading one verse in each set.

Devise Scripture searches so students practice writing Scripture references:

> Hunting for proverbs that they like
>
> Finding the names used for Jesus in a particular gospel
>
> Locating some examples of the humanness of Jesus
>
> Looking for the names of Christian virtues in the epistles
>
> Searching for verses on a certain theme: faith, love, prayer, forgiveness, or mercy

Introduce your students to Bible reference books including a concordance (which lists words and where they occur in the Bible) and the *New Jerome Biblical Commentary* and other commentaries. They can go to www.bible.catholic.net to search for any word in Scripture.

Direct independent reading of Scripture by providing guides for students to use as they read. Ask them to answer simple questions, or finish an incomplete chart, or fill in an outline, or complete a poem with words missing, such as the one based on 1 Samuel 16–26. (See Illustration B in the Appendix.)

Teach your students to mentally replay gospel stories incorporating all their senses. Visualize the scene: the people, the country, the house. Hear the sounds: the words, the voices, and the background noises. Smell the smells, taste the tastes, and feel the sensations. See how this works with the story of the storm at sea:

> He got into a boat, and his disciples followed him. Suddenly a violent storm came upon the sea, so that the boat was being swamped by waves; but he was asleep. They came and woke him, saying, "Lord, save us! We are perishing!" He said to them, "Why are you terrified, O you of little faith?" Then he got up, rebuked the winds and the sea, and there was great calm. The men were amazed and said, "What sort of man is this, whom even the winds and the sea obey?"   » Matthew 8:23–27

Use your imagination and experience to bring these five verses to life. In your mind's eye visualize the storm, the churning gray clouds, the flashes of lightning, the towering waves, the water filling the boat around the men's ankles. Hear the crashes of thunder, the frantic shouts of the men. Feel the soaked clothing, the wild pitching of the boat, the splashes of water. Smell the ozone from the lightning and taste the saltwater running down the men's faces.

Then see someone shaking Jesus and imagine the expression in Jesus' voice as he asks, "Why are you terrified, O you of little faith?" Does he show disappointment, gentle teasing, anger? Hear Jesus telling the wind and waves to be still. Does he shout over the storm, or are his words drowned out by its noise?

Visualize the immediate cessation of the wind and waves. Be aware of the eerie stillness in striking contrast to the deafening noise of the storm. Picture the looks on the faces of the disciples. What would you have done if you had been there? How would you have felt?

Such a vivid recreation of the passage better prepares us to consider the key questions: What strikes me about God in this reading? What is God saying to me?

Give a pretest on a Bible story to pique the students' interest, especially when they think they already know the old, familiar story. Use a multiple choice format and make some of the choices funny like these samples from a quiz on Noah taken from *Teaching the Bible Creatively* by Bill McNabo and Steven Mabry:

> What were the names of Noah's three sons?
> > a. Ham, Shem, and Japheth
> > b. Ham, Sam, and Jeff
> > c. Ham, Turkey, on Rye
> > d. Huey, Dewey, and Louie
>
> Where did the flood waters come from?
> > a. A broken pipe
> > b. The sky
> > c. Inside the earth
> > d. Both b and c

Challenge your students to find the names of books in the Bible hidden in a paragraph. (See Illustration Y in the Appendix on page 134.) Or have them compose such a paragraph and trade with a classmate to solve.

Somehow provide children with subscriptions to *Living Faith Kids*, daily Catholic devotions based on a Scripture passage from the day's Mass, available from Creative Communications for the Parish (1564 Fencorp Drive, Fenton, Missouri 63026-2942).

CHAPTER 2

Proclaim the Good News

It is very important that we teach our students how to proclaim Scripture. Mumbling it, racing through it, or mutilating it is not proclaiming. Once at a parish liturgy, a lector praying the Responsorial Psalm said, "May my tongue cleave to my plate [palate] if I forget you Jerusalem." The picture that image conjured up did nothing for the spirit of prayer!

To prepare students to proclaim the word, you might carry out the activity in Illustration W in the Appendix. Talk about eye contact, enunciation, expression, projection, pronunciation, and poise. Challenge the students to look at the listeners as much as possible. Tell them to let their eyes read ahead of their voice so that they take in strings of words and then recite them without looking at the page.

Encourage students to enunciate and to use expression. Tell them about Demosthenes, a Greek orator who practiced by filling his mouth with marbles. Then, with his mouth full, he tried to speak clearly. Have the students exaggerate as they practice, so that even if stage fright overcomes them, their reading will still be better than before they practiced.

To ensure that they are heard, have the students concentrate on projecting their voices to the person in the farthest corner of the room. Let them practice with a microphone and try adjusting it for themselves. Have them repeat words they stumble over. For real sticklers, direct them to books like *Lector's Guide to Biblical Pronunciation* by Joseph M. Staudacher (Our Sunday Visitor).

Tactfully call attention to those nervous habits that students tend to develop when facing a group: twisting a strand of hair, playing with a button, shaking a leg, clearing their throats, or anything else that will distract from the word.

Tape record the students or even videotape them if possible. Then have them evaluate themselves and one another. Provide opportunities in class for students to proclaim the word (see Chapter 25, "Celebrate Sacred Scripture," page 75). Most of all, be a model for your students by proclaiming any Scripture passage your lesson calls for with reverence, power, and clarity.

CHAPTER 3

Tell Bible Stories

A delightful way to teach Scripture is actually to tell Bible stories. This is, after all, the way Scripture was first handed down. Adults as well as children can be fascinated by the stories in the Bible.

The vocabulary and the content of stories should be adapted to the audience. Children do not need to hear all the details, but they do enjoy updated versions of the stories they've grown up with. For example, in telling the story of the multiplication of the loaves and fish, remark that the nearest fast-food restaurant was a mile away. Flesh out the stories in the Bible when only the skeleton is given. You can do research or use your imagination and common sense to fill in the details. Consult commentaries like the *New Jerome Biblical Commentary* for background information. Imagine yourself in the situations described and notice the surroundings and the expressions on people's faces. Put yourself in the shoes of the main characters and sense their feelings and reactions. Ask questions about what happens.

In preparing to tell the story of the daughter of Jairus, for example, visualize the crowd at the lakeside. See Jairus elbowing his way up to Jesus and then falling at his feet. Feel Jairus' relief as Jesus agrees to go with him, his frustration when Jesus stops to speak to the woman who touched his cloak, and Jairus' despair when he is told that his daughter has died.

Ask yourself: What did Jesus see and hear when he entered Jairus' house? What did the mourners say when they made fun of him? How did he feel as he put them out?

Imagine what the little girl experienced coming back to consciousness and feeling someone holding her hand. Think what it was like for her to open her eyes and see Jesus looking down at her. How did her parents react? What happened after Jesus said, "Give her something to eat" (Mark 5:21–43)?

A story is more effective if you insert dramatic pauses, facial expressions, and gestures, but the success of your presentation is largely determined by your voice: its quality, its pace, and its expression. Before venturing to tell a story, practice until you are very familiar with it. Tell it in front of a mirror or before an honest friend. Tape record your story for a real revelation about your storytelling techniques.

Before telling the story, explain words and concepts that might puzzle the children. State briefly the story that is about to pique their interest, but don't reveal too much.

Here are ten ways to add variety and charm to the telling of a Bible story:

1. Have the children sit on a special storytelling quilt.

2. Introduce the story with a concrete object. The children might pull it out of a pocket or a box.

3. Add sensory words as you tell the stories. For instance if Jesus is in a boat, mention the warm sun, the water lapping, the graceful birds flying.

4. Tell the story through a puppet. Puppets can be purchased or made out of a sock, a mitten, a popsicle stick, a chenille stick, a paper plate, a balloon, a tongue depressor, a one-pint milk carton, or a paper bag.

5. Accompany the story with simple line drawings. Use colored pens/chalk if possible. You might begin with mysterious lines and shapes or unfinished words. You do not have to be a Picasso. In fact, if your art is worse than the students' art, they enjoy it all the more. (See Illustration C in the Appendix for pictures to draw as you tell the parable of the Prodigal Son.)

6. Use cutout figures on the overhead or on a flannel board. Make your own figures and attach a piece of felt to the back so they adhere to a flannel board. High school teachers might borrow a board from primary teachers. A retreat director I know uses a flannel board very successfully in telling stories to adults.

7. Work with another person (a teacher helper) and tell the story as an interview. For instance, have a friend come in as Cinderella and begin scrubbing the floor. Talk about the infant Jesus who was born in a poor stable and was adored by poor shepherds.

8. Tear or fold a piece of paper as you talk, making an object related to the story. For example, as you tell the story of Jonah and the whale, make a whale. (See Illustration D in the Appendix for directions.) The books *Clip and Tell Bible Stories* by Lois Keffer and *Snip and Tell Bible Stories* by Karyn Henley (Group Publishing) contain other patterns.

9. Draw the story in four parts on a transparency or a large sheet of paper. Make a cover sheet by folding a paper in fourths and slitting it along one fold to the center. As you tell the story, uncover one picture at a time, gradually folding up the cover sheet. (See Illustration E in the Appendix for drawings to accompany the story of the lost sheep.)

10. As you retell a story, focus each time on a different sense.

Involve the children as you tell the story:

- Look at the children individually as you speak.
- Draw a child or two into the telling like an entertainer invites a member of the audience to the stage.
- Ask questions during the story to hold interest and stimulate thinking.
- Take the children on a story walk in the room or on the parish property. For instance, as you tell the story of the Good Samaritan, move from the road to the inn. As you tell the story of the paschal mystery, move from the upper room, to the garden of olives, to Pilate's hall, to Calvary, and to the garden of the resurrection.
- Help the children paste pictures on a large sheet of paper as you tell the story.
- Have the children manipulate puppets or figures on a flannel board.
- Let the children draw or work with clay as you tell the story.
- Give children pictures of people or objects in the story and as you mention them, let these children pop up from their seats.
- Invite the children to add key lines, gestures, and sound effects.
- Let the children say a word or do an action when they hear a certain word. As you tell the story of the miraculous catch of fish, the children might say "glub, glub, glub" whenever you say "fish."

To have the children retell a story, have them toss a ball of yarn to one another. Each child who catches the yarn tells a part of the story.

Encourage the students to tell biblical stories to other children: younger brothers and sisters, children they babysit, or children at a daycare center. You might arrange to have your students tell stories to small groups of younger students in another class. You'll be surprised to see how well they imitate you. You might even arrange to have a storytelling festival for the whole school!

CHAPTER 4

Dramatize Scripture Stories

If you want to wake up your students, act out a story from the Bible. To teach the story of the burning bush, dress like Moses, bearded and with staff in hand, and, believe me, you'll have everyone's attention. To demonstrate Peter's Pentecost sermon, one second-grade teacher jumped up on a reading chair and shouted, "Jesus is risen. He's alive!" Then she jumped down again to become a member of the crowd wondering, "What's the matter with them? Are they drunk?" She was very effective.

An alternative to acting out the story yourself is having the students enact it. Children remember best those classes in which they were actively involved. What religion classes from your childhood do you recall best? Probably the ones in which you played a part.

Most students love to act. Some are born hams. The introverts prefer to act out stories using puppets or paper cutouts on the overhead. One shy girl in my class, though, played the apple tree in the Garden of Eden. She just stood there dangling the apple from her fingers, and she stole the show.

Many episodes from both the Old and New Testaments beg to be enacted—from Genesis (Abraham and the visitors, Jacob and Esau, Rebekah, Joseph) to Acts of the Apostles (the death of Stephen, the conversion of Paul, Peter's escape from prison, and the journeys of Paul and Barnabas). Let the children act out the parables, miracles, and other events from the gospels. (See *Gospel Theater for the Whole Community* in "Resources," page 92.) One seventh-grade class produced a program of parable plays that had two narrators (news anchors) introducing each play. The students performed it for their families, and their teacher videotaped it.

Even the youngest child, who can't read or write, can mime a story, put on a shadow play, or stand in place as part of a "living picture" production. Sometimes the entire class can provide actions for a story simultaneously. For example, children love to pretend to be seeds in the Parable of the Seed. They are especially good at being the seeds that are choked to death!

Let older students interview or hold a press conference with the queen of Sheba, or the blind man healed by Jesus, the apostle John, or Lazarus after he was raised from the dead. Have them produce a talk show with Noah and God, or with Saul, David, and Solomon. Help them plan a TV tribute to Joshua, who led the Hebrews into the promised land, or the boy who handed over his loaves and fish, or Joseph of Arimathea, who gave his tomb for Jesus' burial. They can stage a courtroom scene where witnesses declare Jesus is alive based on the post-resurrection stories. Let them prepare commercials or sixty-second radio spots with a prophetic message or a piece of "Good News."

Have them write and present a play about Esther and invite the audience to applaud the heroes and hiss the villains (or use noisemakers to show their dislike) as the Jewish people do at Purim when the story of Esther is part of their celebration. Encourage the students to use costumes, props, and taped sound effects and to draw scenery on the blackboard. (See Illustration F in the Appendix for a play about Esther.) Younger children's roles can be identified by sandwich boards, headbands, or vests made from grocery bags.

For variety in dramatizing the Bible, use choral reading. Have groups of students each recite a Beatitude, or direct small groups to chime in during the recitation of Psalm 150 for a cumulative effect. Rewrite a passage in Scripture so that the story is told by characters alternating with a chorus. Include directions for the voices like "strong," "soft," "echoing," or "gruff." (See Illustration G in the Appendix for a sample choral reading about Abraham.)

Children can experience the psalms as liturgy by praying them in different ways. Divide the class into two sides and have them alternate praying sections of a psalm. Psalms that are easily prayed with students this way are Psalms 1, 4, 19, 33, 56, 63, 86, 92, 112, and 139. Another way to pray the psalms is to have a reader pray a psalm, with the class repeating an antiphon after each verse or section. Psalms and suggested antiphons for this method are:

Psalm 16: I trust in you, O Lord.

Psalm 29: Praise the Lord.

Psalm 91: You are my defender.

Psalm 96: The Lord is king.

Psalm 100: Alleluia, alleluia.

Psalm 138: I thank you, Lord.

Psalm 147: Sing praise to our God.

Perform an echo pantomime. Tell each line of the story with a movement. The children repeat each line and the movement. A variation is the "wave" pantomime. Children stand in a line next to each other and repeat the words and actions one by one.

THE LOST COIN

Once a woman had ten coins.
[Hold up ten fingers.]

One day one was missing.
[Fold over a thumb.]

She looked and looked.
[Hold hand above eyes and look from side to side.]

She swept her house.
[Make sweeping motions.]

She found her coin.
[Hold up hand with the thumb and index finger together.]

The woman ran to get her friends.
[Run in place.]

And they celebrated.
[Jump up and down, waving arms in air.]

CHAPTER 5

Relate Scripture to the World

By relating the Bible to contemporary situations, we help our students to conclude that it is grounded in reality, that it mirrors common human experiences, and that it has a message for us now.

We might well ask, How can this book written by people in a totally different culture about two thousand years ago have meaning for us? The answer is that it is a classic—a book that continues to have meaning for people. People continue to respond to its message. The meaning of Scripture is not frozen; it's alive and so is the Spirit working in the midst of the Church community today. The Bible has meaning for us as we deal with computers and cell phones, AIDS, the economy, and the crisis in families.

To help students understand this concept, show a piece of art. Ask for a title for the artwork, and then reveal the actual title. Point out to the students how their culture and immediate circumstances led them to find particular meanings. (A good picture for this demonstration is one by Kathe Kollwitz which shows an adult embracing or shielding children. Suggested titles are usually related to God but also to current issues such as abortion and the most recent natural disaster. The real title is "The Seed Corn Must Not Be Sown." Farmers don't plant all their seed in one year. They save some for the future in case the annual crop is lost. Kathe Kollwitz lost two sons in World War I. She lived in Nazi Germany and was warning against World War II.)

Have the students comb the newspapers for modern-day characters and events that are similar to ones in the Bible. Encourage them to find a modern-day Job, Judas, or Paul, and perhaps a new Exodus, Exile, or crucifixion. When teaching the gospels, have the students ask people what Jesus means to them today, or ask the students to give concrete examples of people they know who live the Beatitudes.

Relate the people in the Bible to your students and their own lives. Let them see that Adam and Eve progressed through the same stages of sin that they do: being attracted to it, questioning the commandment, entertaining the idea, yielding to temptation, being ashamed, and then being alienated from God. Point out that just as Abraham was called to a journey of faith, so are they. Show how the beautiful friendship between David and Jonathan can be a model for their own relationships. Help them to identify with impetuous Peter, who was brash and disloyal, but who also loved Jesus.

Plan experiences for the students that link their lives to the lives of biblical characters. For example, when teaching about Hosea and his unfaithful wife, Gomer, lead students in a discussion about family and the ingredients of true love. Ask them to write a letter in Hosea's name to Dear Abby, or invite them to compose a love poem, as Hosea might have written it.

To further personalize the Bible, have the students read certain verses and give an example of what they mean for someone their age. Read psalms to them and ask them to suggest appropriate times when these might be used for prayer. Suggest that they try to answer the questions that Jesus asked people:

What do you want me to do for you? (Matthew 20:32)

And you, who do you say that I am? (Matthew 16:15)

What are you looking for? (John 1:38)

Do you want to be well? (John 5:6)

Why are you so terrified, O you of little faith? (Matthew 8:26)

Whoever lives and believes in me will never die. Do you believe this? (John 11:26, *Jerusalem Bible*)

Have I been with you all this time, *Name*, and you still do not know me? (John 14:9, *Jerusalem Bible*)

Have students bring in their family Bible, show it, and talk about how their family uses it.

To introduce literary forms of the Bible, draw parallels with things familiar to the students. Compare them to newspaper sections or the different kinds of books in a library. The proverbs are like bumper stickers, buttons, or posters. The Song of Songs is like a love song. The epistles are like letters we receive today from our bishop. The parables Jesus told are like Aesop's fables.

When the opportunity arises, relate aspects of the Jewish faith in the Bible to the practices of Jewish people today: the celebration of feast days like Passover (the Exodus), Hanukkah (the rededication of the Temple by Judas Maccabeus), and Purim (liberation through Esther); the Sabbath; the shema (Deuteronomy 6:4–5), which is prayed every day; and dietary laws. Invite a rabbi or a Jewish person to speak to the students about the Hebrew Scriptures. You might even plan a field trip to a synagogue.

One project that could involve the whole family is to have the students compile a photo album and then use verses from the Book of Psalms as captions. Apply the Bible to issues that concern them. For instance, in discussing drinking have the students read and discuss John 2:1–11 (the wedding at Cana), Luke 7:33–35, Romans 13:13, 1 Corinthians 6:9–10, Galatians 5:19–21, Ecclesiastes 10:19, and 1 Timothy 5:23.

When telling Scripture stories incorporate modern images and analogies. For example, remark that Goliath was taller than Shaquille O'Neal.

The main way that adult Catholics are in touch with Scripture is in the Sunday liturgies. Teach your students the practice of gleaning one significant verse from the Sunday liturgy to focus on during the week. They can post this verse, pray it, reflect on it, and use it in family prayers throughout the week.

Present Scripture prayers and passages and ask the students when it would be appropriate to pray them. Or give the students a list like the following and have them tell why each reference would be good for its situation.

> When I am troubled or confused • JOHN 14:27
>
> When I think of death • JOHN 11:21–26
>
> When I am in trouble • MATTHEW 11:28–30
>
> When someone has hurt me • MATTHEW 18:21–35
>
> When I have hurt someone • MATTHEW 5:23–24
>
> When I am afraid or worried • MARK 4:35–41
>
> When I want more than I have • LUKE 21:1–4
>
> When a friend has disappointed me • LUKE 6:36–38
>
> When I wonder if anyone loves me • JOHN 19:28–30
>
> When I am happy • PSALM 23; PSALM 148; PHILIPPIANS 4:4–7
>
> When I am thankful • PSALM 138; LUKE 17:11–19
>
> When I am frightened • LUKE 12:32; JOHN 14:1–4
>
> When I need love • JOHN 15:15; PHILIPPIANS 1:7–9; ISAIAH 43:1–4
>
> When I am discouraged • JOHN 16:22, 33; MATTHEW 6:28–34
>
> When I need forgiveness • MATTHEW 9:6–13; MARK 11:24–25; PSALM 51

When I need healing • JAMES 5:13–16; MARK 5:35–43

When I have deep sorrow • 2 CORINTHIANS 12:8–9; PHILIPPIANS 2:13

When I feel hopeless • MARK 15:34; PSALM 13:1; PSALM 91:1, 5

When I face a challenge • PHILIPPIANS 4:13; ISAIAH 6:8; EXODUS 3:11–12

When I am lonely • MARK 14:37; ACTS 17:28; MATTHEW 28:20

When I fail • MARK 15:34; EPHESIANS 3:20–21; 2 CORINTHIANS 12:7

When I am exhausted • 1 CORINTHIANS 10:13; PSALM 69:1, 4; 2 CORINTHIANS 12:7

When I am envious • 1 JOHN 2:15–17; HEBREWS 13:14; 2 CORINTHIANS 12:7–9

Through efforts like these, your students will gradually come to interpret their lives and their world through God's word.

CHAPTER 6

Correlate Scripture with the Arts

It's essential that you try to correlate Scripture with other subjects. For example, supplement your lessons with literature. Many catechists have discovered the power of *The Velveteen Rabbit* by Margery Williams, or *The Giving Tree* by Shel Silverstein to reinforce a lesson. For guidance in finding appropriate books, refer to publications like *Trailing Clouds of Glory* by Madeleine L'Engle (Westminster Press). Your public library has at least one hefty guide to children's literature. Reading from a book for five minutes at the beginning of each class serves to settle the children. Even high school students will anticipate these five minutes if the book is well chosen.

In addition to children's books and adolescent literature, poetry, plays, and short stories also echo biblical themes. James Weldon Johnson's poem "The Creation" is a strong and moving interpretation of the Genesis story. The short story "The Gift of the Magi" by O. Henry is a beautiful expression of the Christmas themes of love and sacrifice. Archibald MacLeish's play *J.B.* can give older students insights into the story of Job.

Introduce music into your scriptural lessons: classical and popular, religious and secular. Analyze popular songs to see whether they contradict or support gospel values. Play classical pieces while the children do independent or group work, as a stimulus or background for prayer, or as an approach to a lesson. Make use of old hymns like "Amazing Grace" and also contemporary Christian songs. Christmas carols contain enough theology to teach the facts and the meaning of the infancy narratives, while Handel's *Messiah* is a glorious prelude to a lesson on Easter. (See "Music" in Resources on page 95.)

Use art masterpieces. Tell the story of Mary's life or the last days of Jesus through slides or a PowerPoint presentation of famous paintings. Take a field trip to an art museum to see paintings depicting biblical events or visit the history museum to find artifacts from biblical times. Introduce your students to icons.

In the Middle Ages illiterate people learned Bible stories through stained-glass windows. Have your students study those in your church. Or bring pictures of some to class.

Use pictures, posters, and photos to begin or summarize a lesson or to evoke a Scripture-based prayer. You might give each student a small picture or display a large one. Show several interpretations of the same topic and discuss their similarities and differences: the Annunciation, the Last Supper, the Crucifixion, the Good Shepherd. Direct students to www.religionfacts. com and have them click on "Jesus" and then "Jesus Image Gallery" to view a hundred images of Jesus.

Older students will enjoy learning the rudiments of calligraphy so that they can letter Scripture verses in the manner of the early manuscripts. Have them use calligraphy pens. Penpoints from the C series work well. India ink is the best medium, but watercolor paint applied to the points with a brush can be substituted. Another alternative is to use felt-tipped pens with points shaped for lettering. Instruct the students to keep their paper straight in front of them and to hold the pen at a forty-five degree angle at all times. Suggest that they hold their breath while making long, straight strokes. Give them a model sheet of the alphabet. (See Illustration H in the Appendix.)

Show the students volumes of the *St. John's Bible*. These are handwritten and beautifully illuminated under the direction of Donald Jackson, official scribe of Queen Elizabeth II (Liturgical Press).

CHAPTER 7

Share the Personal Impact of Scripture

Faith is contagious. As a believing Christian, you have more impact on your students than any textbook series or audiovisual could ever have. It's no surprise then that a key technique in teaching Scripture is personal sharing. Be willing to share what the Bible means to you. Tell about a time that you discovered something new in a passage, or a time when verses had a specific meaning for you. In Jeremiah 23:29, God asks, "Is not my word like fire…like a hammer shattering rocks?" Ask students if a Scripture passage has ever been like lightning streaking through them, or like a hammer that God hits them over the head with.

Your sharing can be integrated into teacher-student interaction during the development of a lesson, or it can be part of a celebration or prayer service. It can even take the form of comments on the papers of individual students.

Saint Augustine let us know that his conversion was attributed to Scripture. As he sat under a tree, he heard a child's voice repeating, "Take and read." He opened the Bible, and God overtook him. Francis of Assisi shared his experience of Scripture with his brothers. Tradition says that when he opened the Bible at random three times, the verses he found became the foundation for the Franciscan community. Saint Francis called this technique the First Opening. Some people call it the Lucky Dip or Bible Roulette. When Thomas Merton was discerning whether or not to become a Trappist, he opened his Bible to the psalms and his eyes fell on the words, "Be silent" in Psalm 46. More recently, the singer and composer John Michael Talbot used the same process to come to a decision during a crisis point in his life. The story is related in his biography *Troubadour for the Lord* by Dan O'Neill (Crossroad Publishing Company).

Before teaching this way of being open to God's word, remind the students that God is present in the words of Scripture and that God's word is meant for them. Encourage them to expect God to speak directly to them in certain verses.

In discussing the Gospel story of the woman who was cured by touching Jesus' cloak, Louis Evely wrote in his book *That Man Is You*:

> Now everybody'd touched Him, everybody'd hustled Him, still nobody'd been cured or transformed. Only one had touched Him with faith; and a profound sense of well-being coursed through her; she was cured. As for us, we all read the Gospels now and then. But if we approach them like an ordinary book they'll produce no extraordinary effect on us. We have to read them the way we'd have touched Christ: with the same reverence, the same faith, the same expectancy.

With this kind of guidance, our students will learn to read Scripture not merely with their minds, but with their hearts.

I'd like to share here one of my personal experiences with God's word.

> I entered the convent in the sixties, a time of great upheaval. The very year I entered, the Sisters I had idolized began leaving left and right. I began to wonder if I should leave, too. One day I was alone in chapel with desperate thoughts running through my mind like, "What am I doing here? Religious life is falling apart. Help, Lord! What am I supposed to do?" Since no one was around, I walked up to the Bible enthroned in the front of the chapel. I looked down at the page, and the words of Matthew 19:29 (*Jerusalem Bible* translation) leaped out at me: "And everyone who has left houses, brothers, sisters, father, mother, children, or land for the sake of my name will be repaid a hundred times over and also inherit eternal life." I stayed. Some may call it just a coincidence, but for me that day, God spoke.

Granted, sharing your personal experiences may be uncomfortable and risky, especially if some students (or the whole class!) give you problems. Nevertheless, for the sake of those students who will be touched by your self-disclosure, dare to do it!

Invariably your sharing of personal stories, like this one of mine, will spark student sharing. And everyone will leave class with a stronger faith, maybe you more than anyone else, after hearing your students' experiences.

CHAPTER 8

Rewrite Scripture

One way to give students insight into Scripture is to have them rewrite it. For example, suggest that they put the Prodigal Son story in a twenty-first-century setting. The Good Samaritan parable is easier to identify with if you relate it to a driver stranded on the highway who is ignored by people whose bumper stickers read: "Honk if you love Jesus" and rescued by a heavily tattooed and pierced man in a beat-up truck.

The psalms, too, are suitable for rewriting, including the laments. Here is Psalm 23, the Good Shepherd psalm, as rewritten by a student:

> God is my world. With him I don't need nothing [sic].
>
> He helps me to be calm. He keeps me out of trouble.
>
> He makes me live. He keeps me cool for him.
>
> Even though it's dark around me, he makes me unafraid.
>
> Bad things don't scare me because he is with me.
>
> His hands keep everything all right. He has my life mapped out.
>
> He makes me brave in front of people who hate me.
>
> He blesses me. My joy explodes.

Have the students rewrite Psalm 23 based on an image of God other than that of a good shepherd. Alfredo chose to compare God to a counselor. He ended with, "Best of all, God's services are free!"

Besides parables and psalms, students can write their own commandments, proverbs, beatitudes, and accounts of creation.

Passages that lend themselves especially well to paraphrase are Proverbs 31:10–31 (the ideal wife), Habakkuk 3:17–19 (having faith in times of trouble), Luke 1:46–55 (the Magnificat), and 1 Corinthians 13 (the hymn to charity).

Students might also supply "unwritten chapters" of Scripture, for example, Adam's and Eve's reactions to the murder of Abel, Noah's explanation of the ark, episodes from the hidden life of Jesus, and Mary's life after Pentecost.

Bible stories can be recast in the form of plays or poems. Students can write couplets, haiku, ballads, free verse, raps, and limericks. (Donald R. Bensen's *Biblical Limericks*, published in 1986, is composed entirely of limericks on the Old Testament.) See Illustration O in the Appendix for some forms of poems that students might write.

Stories can be retold in informal modern language or in a particular dialect: southern or western. (See Illustration I in the Appendix for a sample recast Bible story called "Genesis According to Room 21.") Older students might rewrite a story as a children's book.

Challenge the students to rewrite a story using words that begin with the same letter. For instance, *Teaching the Bible Creatively* by Bill McNabb and Steven Mabry offers the poem "Melody in F" about the prodigal son. It begins:

> Feeling footloose and frisky, a feather-brained fellow
> Forced his fond father to fork over the farthings,
> And flew far to foreign fields
> And frittered his fortune feasting fabulously with faithless friends.

A powerful prayer technique is to rewrite a story from the Gospel to include yourself. These are the steps:

1. Read a story about Jesus.

2. Rewrite it from a first-person point of view, describing the events as though you were there participating. At the end arrange the situation so that you and Jesus are alone.

3. Conclude with a dialogue between you and Jesus, discussing what happened. Your conversation will lead into thoughts and feelings about yourself and what is going on in your own life.

CHAPTER 9

Research Biblical Topics

Recommend books and articles to your students that throw light on Scripture, for example, *God's Smuggler* by Brother Andrew, and *Hiding Place* by Corrie ten Boom. Introduce them to magazines like *The Bible Today* and *Biblical Archaeology Review*.

Develop in them the habit of independent study. You might have the students choose partners, and each day or week have them report to each other anything new they discovered in the Bible. Or they could report to the whole class.

Students *and* catechists can always learn more about the Bible. Recently I read that after Noah went into the ark, Yahweh closed the door behind him. I had never noticed that detail in the Bible story. I looked it up and there it was: "And Yahweh closed the door behind Noah." Even more recently I learned about Bible codes. Using computers scholars discovered that equally spaced letters in the Orthodox Hebrew Bible spell related words going forwards or backwards. For example, every fourth letter in a verse may spell "Jesus," while every sixth letter may spell "Messiah." Words related to events like the crucifixion, the Holocaust, and the Oklahoma City bombing have been found clustered together.

I thought I knew Psalm 23 until I read the book *A Shepherd Looks at Psalm 23* by Phillip Keller (Zondervan) and learned about "cast sheep." A cast sheep is a sheep that has turned over on its back and can't get up again. It struggles frantically and is vulnerable to attack. Gases build up in the rumen of the sheep and cut off circulation to the extremities. In the summer a sheep can die in a few hours. If it's cool, the agony can last several days. A good shepherd is always on the watch for cast sheep. When he finds one, he rolls it over and lifts it onto its feet. Then he straddles it and holds it upright, rubbing its limbs to restore circulation, all the while speaking to it encouragingly. It takes a long time to restore a cast down sheep. This concept gave me a new appreciation of the good shepherd who "restoreth my soul."

Assign reports on the Bible. Some possible topics:

The process of the composition of the Bible

Deuterocanonical books

Apocryphal books

Translations of the Bible

Versions like the Thumb Bible, the Vinegar Bible, the Wicked Bible, and the Devil's Bible

The peoples of the Bible

The Israelites' life in biblical times: customs, food, clothing, shelter, coins, measurements of time

Palestine

Archaeological finds like the Dead Sea Scrolls

Jewish feasts

The evangelists: their audiences, styles, and symbols

The Hebrew alphabet

Number symbolism in the Bible

Bible codes discovered recently

Acquaint your students with handbooks of the Bible, dictionaries and encyclopedias of the Bible, and concordances.

Homilies are Scripture-based. Have your students discuss what new insights they received from a homily on a particular day. Let them compare the differences in the homilies, if they heard different preachers.

Invite students to ask people they know what their favorite book of the Bible is or their favorite biblical story. Have them search for the role of the Bible in the lives of famous men and women.

More advanced students can read the *Constitution on Divine Revelation*, whole or in part, and do a report on their findings. (See Illustration J in the Appendix for a study guide that can be used with this Constitution. It is based on the collection of documents edited by Austin Flannery, OP [Costello Publishing Company]).

Keep in mind that the goal of Bible study is to know Jesus, not to be Bible experts. A deaf person can read music but never hears it. We don't want our students to be like that.

CHAPTER 10

Create Scriptural Artwork

If it's true that we remember twenty percent of what we hear and ninety percent of what we do, then time spent in creative activity is time well spent. Let the students translate the word of Scripture into art, sometimes working in groups to foster community. Plan for them to experience different media—from fingerpaint to crayons on sandpaper. They might draw on a styrofoam cup or an old window shade. For a simple and clean art activity, let the children draw on the blackboard with water. For an outside activity, sidewalk art done with chalk brings joy to artists and observers alike.

Scriptural verses can be lettered on posters, buttons, banners, balloons, mobiles, bumper stickers, bookmarks, placemats, holy cards, pennants, seashells, driftwood, doorknob hangers (tagboard with a hole and a slit at the top), all-occasion greeting cards, scrolls, pencil holders, brick bookends or doorstops, stationery, T-shirts, paperweights made from rocks, and wooden plaques coated with shellac. To heighten student interest in these projects, teach calligraphy. (See Chapter 6, "Correlate Scripture with the Arts," page 24.)

Students can use their ingenuity to design book jackets, album covers for CDs, posters, bulletin boards, banners, billboards, commemorative stamps, postcards, calendars, windsocks, windshield flyers, logos, and even quilts, based on a biblical book or theme. They can fill a display case with an exhibit on the prophets or on the parables. Banners can be hung in the school hall or the church. Each child can hang a personal banner from the front of his or her desk.

Biblical stories can be illustrated in many ways. Children can make huge murals of creation, Jesus' miracles, or his last days. They can make tiny pictures out of their fingerprints, using colored ink pads and filling in details with felt-tipped pens. They can present a story in the form of a torn-paper picture, a yarn and cloth picture, a tryptich (a three-paneled picture), a cartoon or comic strip, a time capsule, photos, a collage of magazine pictures, a comic book, or a children's storybook. They can wrap cardboard with foil, paint it completely with tempera, and then scratch a picture onto the foil. Two ninth-graders created a needlepoint picture of the days of creation that included "God rested" as a head with "Z-Z-Z" above it.

Freehand drawings from all the children can be compiled into one class booklet. This can be the conventional bound booklet (stapled or tied with yarn) or the accordion type. Laminate the best drawings and use them to tell biblical stories in the future. The young artists will be proud when you ask to keep their work, and other classes will be delighted to see children's art while they listen to a story.

You might give your students a story with spaces for certain words that are objects. Direct them to finish the story by drawing art for the missing words.

People of the Bible become unforgettable when children reflect on them and their lives in an attempt to represent them. They can design a coat of arms for Abraham, Gideon, Peter, or Paul. They can cut silhouettes of various people in a story or make paper cutout dolls that have sets of clothes. They might make puppets out of paper bags, paper plates, paper towel tubes, or small raisin or gelatin boxes on a stick, socks, clothespins, or simply by pasting paper figures on the end of a pencil. Children who are artistic might enjoy making a portfolio of biblical portraits using pen and ink, watercolor, or pastels. Brief character descriptions can accompany portraits of the patriarchs, heroines of the Bible, or the apostles. The students might create an illustrated biography of one person.

Art projects for the more ambitious catechist and students can be planned in class and then carried out at home. Abraham's sacrifice of Isaac or the Annunciation can be portrayed in wire sculpture, aluminum foil, or papier-mâché. Dioramas made with shoe boxes are suited to scenes with more than two characters: the Stations of the Cross, or colorful stories like Daniel in the lions' den, or Peter walking on the water. Scenery is crayoned or painted on the inside of the box, and figures and props are made to stand by means of pipe cleaners or tabs glued to the bottom of the box.

Bible characters and objects can be made from paper strips fastened together.

Patient students can devise a tab-pull book. One boy depicted the Exodus this way. His first page shows a basket in reeds. When the tab is pulled, the basket goes across the water. His second page shows a bush. When the tab at the top is pulled, flames leap up from it. The third page shows a sea. When the tab at the right is pulled, the sea parts to reveal people. The fourth page shows a cloud above the Israelites. When the tab is pulled, the cloud moves, leading the people through the desert.

Mobiles with symbols related to a biblical book or theme create a joyful atmosphere in a classroom. These can be made from multidimensional figures decorated with drawn pictures, magazine pictures, or construction-paper symbols and suspended from a hanger. Use different shapes, sizes, and colors.

A pop-up picture can be made by affixing accordion-pleated strips of paper to the backs of figures and attaching the base of the strips to a completed scene.

Stained-glass windows can be designed simply by drawing a picture on paper and lacing it with thick black lines. For a more realistic effect, paste tissue paper on strips of black construction paper. A group of students can transform an entire bulletin board into a stained-glass window of the Good Shepherd, the Passion, or a patron saint.

Mosaic, a form of religious art popular in the fourth century, can be created using large or small pieces of construction paper or colored sections of magazine pages. For different effects, students can use paper punch holes (picked up and put in place with a straight pin), Easter egg shells, or a mixture of seeds, popcorn, lentils, split peas, black beans, kidney beans, noodles, and rice.

Students can construct models of the Ark of the Covenant, Solomon's Temple, or the Holy Land. They can use clay to shape a braided cross with toothpick thorns, a manger, a cross, or symbols for Moses, David, or Mary. Or, use bread dough:

> Thoroughly mix: 4 cups flour, 1 cup salt, 1½ cups water

> After the children have molded their symbols, bake at 350° until hardened. (Large pieces may take up to an hour.)

Boxes (shoe boxes or tissue cubes) can be decorated on each side according to a theme: a glory box, an Easter box, a joy box, a box on the Works of Mercy. Or you may wish to have younger children make a religion box to hold all their art projects at home. Their parents might appreciate this.

Medallions that can be pinned on or worn around the neck can be designed from clay or cardboard.

Magnets for refrigerators and other metallic surfaces can be created by gluing artwork to magnetic material. The magnetic backing comes in sheets or rolls and can be cut to the desired size and shape.

Psalm verses can be creatively designed. Letters can be illuminated. Words can be drawn to symbolize what they represent. For instance, for "The Lord is my rock," the "o" in rock can be drawn as a rock with grass.

Photo essays made with magazine pictures or students' own photographs are something they will want to keep. One of the psalms or Jesus' Sermon on the Mount would make good subjects. Students can also put together mock photo albums of a particular family in the Bible, for example, Abraham's family or the family of King David. They can draw original illustrations and write captions for each "photo."

The class might work together to make an illustrated timeline.

During Advent a small Christmas tree can become a Jesse tree, containing symbols of the people and events associated with the Messiah. The tree takes its name from Isaiah 11:1, "Thus saith the Lord God: There shall come forth a rod out of the root of Jesse, and a flower shall rise up out of his root." Jesse was the father of King David. The students can create the symbols from paper or from other materials and objects. (See Illustrations K and L in the Appendix for some sample Jesse tree symbols and a Jesse tree.) In place of a real tree you might draw one on a large sheet of paper, outline one with green yarn on a bulletin board or a display board, or set branches in plaster of Paris.

A parallel Advent activity is the more recent custom of making a Chrismon tree (Christ + monogram). The Chrismon tree bears symbols of Jesus from the New Testament. While the children hang their symbols, related Scripture texts might be read. Possible figures for the Chrismon tree are Mary, Joseph, the star, manger, shepherd, angel, sheep, three kings, gifts, fish, dove, grapes, wheat, vine, crown, rock, alpha and omega symbols, Chi-Rho, anchor, and cross. The symbols are usually white and gold.

Have younger students color pictures of Bible stories. Typing "Bible coloring pages" in a search engine will yield numerous sites that offer free pictures. These can be printed, or students can color some on the computer. Pictures on some sites are cartoonish or too few. A particularly good site is www.bible-printables.com.

Help students make a flip book on a Bible event. On small papers they draw pictures, each with little progressive changes so that when the papers are stapled at one end and flipped with the thumb, the scene appears to be moving.

When students do creative activities, keep in mind that the end product is not as important as the process!

CHAPTER 11

Add Humor to Scripture Study

Laughter is good. Jesus' death and resurrection give us reason to face today and tomorrow with joy. Our church, therefore, has the potential to be a laughing church. In *The Little Prince* by Antoine de Saint Exupéry, the Little Prince leaves his friend the gift of laughter. We can give our children the gift of laughter, too. Joy, one of the fruits of the Holy Spirit, should mark our teaching of the Good News.

As we read Scripture, we should be attuned to the divine sense of humor. Alert your students to the fun in the Noah story with its animal parade. (Bill Cosby's version can be found on the Internet.) Children will enjoy knowing that the Jonah story has a man-eating whale and a plant-eating worm. Recall for them, too, the humor in the predicament of Peter as he slips into the sea after walking on the water. Then, too, there's the comical episode of Jesus spotting the short Zacchaeus among the sycamore leaves. The story about Jesus arranging for tax money to appear in the mouth of a fish is as much a practical joke as a miracle. Also, when Jesus says that it is as difficult for a rich man to get into heaven as for a camel to go through the eye of a needle, the comparison is preposterous and funny, especially if the camel is Bactrian (two-humped)!

The humor continues through Acts. Rhoda is so excited to see Peter at the door that she runs to tell everyone of his arrival and forgets to let him in. And then there is Eutychus who dozes during one of Paul's sermons and falls out of the window. We can laugh at that because, luckily, Paul was able to bring him back to life.

Good speakers know the secret of sprinkling their talks with jokes and funny anecdotes to keep their audience with them. Catechists can employ this secret to sustain interest and to create a happy atmosphere. In the Bible itself we find the words "A joyful heart is the health of the body, but a depressed spirit dries up the bones" (Proverbs 17:22).

It's a good idea to jot down jokes related to Scripture when you read or hear them. Here is a start for your collection:

Adam and Eve One day Adam and Eve and their two boys were walking past the gates of Paradise, which was guarded by the cherubim. Abel inquired, "What's that, Dad?"

Adam replied, "That's where we used to live before your mother ate us out of house and home."

Lot's Wife A teacher was telling the story of the flight of Lot's family from Sodom. When she got to the part where Lot's wife looked back and turned into a pillar of salt, one child remarked, "That's nothing. Once my mother looked back and turned into a telephone pole."

Exodus/Biblical Truth When Jimmy came home from religion class, his mother asked, "What did you learn today, Jimmy?"

He said, "God sent Moses to rescue the Israelites. When they came to the Red Sea, Moses had engineers build a pontoon bridge. As the Israelites crossed they saw the Egyptian tanks coming. So Moses radioed headquarters to send bombers…"

"Jimmy," interrupted his mother, "is that really what your teacher said?"

"Well, not exactly," he replied. "But if I told it her way, you'd never believe it."

The Possessed Man When Jesus exorcised the possessed man and sent the devils into the pigs, that was the first recorded instance of deviled ham.

The Prodigal Son Reviewing the role of the "other son" in the story of the prodigal son, the teacher said, "There was someone who was not happy at the thought of the feast and who had no desire to go to it. Who was this?"

A small voice piped up, "The fatted calf."

Lazarus One teacher was trying to convey that Jesus had emotions like us while she was telling the story of the death of Lazarus. She said to her four-year-olds, "Jesus did the same thing we do when someone dies. What do we do?"

A child answered, "Call 911."

CHAPTER 12

Sing Scripture-Based Songs

When we teach children to sing biblical songs, snatches will come back to them for the rest of their lives. Not only is singing "praying twice," but it has the power to create an *esprit de corps* among the children. It's a real community experience, especially if the song involves harmony. Songs can be used as prayers to open the class. They can be inserted in the course of a lesson for a change of pace. They also make a good vehicle for the children's response of gratitude and praise at the close of a class. If your voice sounds like a cat with its tail caught in the door, use CDs or enlist the help of a talented colleague or student, but let the children sing.

Find musical arrangements of Scripture and teach them. The psalms are song-prayers. They are meant to be sung. Read *The Catholic Companion to the Psalms* (ACTA Publications) for more information about them. Many contemporary Christian albums contain songs with lyrics that are either direct words of Scripture or based on Scripture. Many of these have catchy melodies that bring the gospel stories to life and present God's message in a lucid and memorable way. Such music is available at Christian bookstores.

Encourage even those students who are not blessed with angelic voices. You might tell them what Thomas à Kempis said: "If you cannot sing like the nightingale and the lark, then sing like the crows and frogs, who sing as God meant them to."

We can do music ministers a service by teaching songs for liturgy. You might consult your music minister to find out the songs he or she would like to add to the school or parish repertoire.

Little children love to sing songs with gestures. Make them up, or let them make them up. High school students can be challenged to write original scriptural songs. They can write ballads about biblical personages or events, e.g., The Ballad of Joseph, Son of Jacob; the Ballad of the Great Escape (Exodus); the Ballad of Mary Magdalene. They can set the psalms to music or compose meditation songs on the sayings of Jesus. They can write parodies and sing them, such as the following:

SAMSON

(To the tune of "Yankee Doodle")

Samson, Samson, mighty champion,

Samson, with your long hair

You can beat the Philistines,

But of their women beware.

MUSTARD SEED

(To the tune of "Twinkle, Twinkle Little Star")

Tiny, tiny mustard seed,

You are small but great indeed.

You will be the largest tree.

Many nests in you we'll see.

Tiny, tiny mustard seed,

You are small but great indeed.

Those students who play musical instruments can be invited to accompany the singing in class celebrations or parish liturgies. In this way they will form the habit of sharing their gifts with the community.

You might have your students draw a picture to a song as it is played or make a book of illustrations corresponding to the song's lyrics.

For a memorable activity, put on a theme-based concert for the school, parents, or parish, for example, a Marian concert or a Christmas concert.

In addition to songs found in your parish hymnal, recommended collections are found under "Resources" (page 95).

CHAPTER 13

Dance in Response to Scripture

At a Mass in Hawaii I once saw a woman do the hula to a communion reflection song. It was a beautiful, graceful act of worship. Choreograph Scripture verses so that the children are able to involve their whole bodies in response to God's word. Devise steps for some scripturally based songs. Play music and let the children invent their own dances. They might do one called "I Love Creation," or "The Dance of the Healed Lepers," or another called "Rejoicing over the Lost Sheep." To allow for more freedom of movement, hold the class in the gym or outside.

Teach simple psalm verses by heart with gestures, perhaps the psalm responses so they will recognize them at Mass: "I thank you, Lord, (raise hands) with all my heart (cross heart)" (Psalm 138:1).

Older students are good at working out liturgical movements for songs. In particular, those students who have had dancing lessons can be called upon to do an interpretive dance of a biblical passage. For wider participation, students can add rhythm instruments, tambourines, drums, or simply clap their hands to the music. (See Illustration M in the Appendix for sample dance movements to accompany the Our Father.)

Akin to dancing is cheerleading. Let students work out routines for Bible events, e.g., a pyramid formation in a mime interpretation of the tower of Babel, a chant with motions for the battle of Jericho, or a cheer about the Beatitudes.

Children dancing can provide high-level entertainment for a school celebration or program. In addition it can enhance a First Communion Mass, a Scripture reading, or a psalm response. Dancing is in line with biblical tradition: Miriam, Moses' sister, danced after the Israelites safely passed through the Red Sea, and David danced before the Ark of the Covenant. At the wedding feast of Cana, Jesus and Mary probably danced with their relatives and friends.

CHAPTER 14

Memorize to Master the Material

Once at a eucharistic celebration, I heard a reader proclaim the entire first reading by heart. It was very striking. With a little prodding, our students are capable of similar feats.

Wary of the pitfalls of the Baltimore Catechism era, modern catechists might be reluctant to have their students memorize anything. But Pope John Paul II pointed out in *Catechesis in Our Time* that "The blossoms…of faith and piety do not grow in the desert places of a memoryless catechesis" (55).

It is good for children to memorize Scripture, especially key verses, Jesus' words, psalms, and other prayers. In the process of memorizing a passage, they often arrive at a deeper understanding of it. Moreover, as with songs, biblical verses once memorized that run through our minds can lead us into prayer. They will also surface when the children need them. For instance, St. Teresa got through serious illness clinging to a verse from Job: "We receive good from God's hand, should we not also receive evil?" Those words saw her through months of pain. Janaan Manternach calls memorizing verses "banking prayers." It is good to provide our students with a rich supply of such verses. They might even memorize the references too.

Actually, many children enjoy memorizing. It gives them a feeling of accomplishment to be able to rattle off the names of the twelve apostles and the fruits of the Holy Spirit (Galatians 5:22–23) or to recite the Beatitudes (Matthew 5:3–10).

In the time of Jesus, scrolls of the Old Testament were kept in synagogues, not homes. When Jesus prayed from Scripture on a mountain and during the night, he relied on his memory.

There are several ways to encourage the memorization of Scripture:

- Teach the students to post a verse of the week on a refrigerator, mirror, or dresser.

- Post charts marking the progress of each student.

- Every week write a verse to be memorized on the board or letter it and display it on the bulletin board.

- Write a verse on the board. Erase one word or phrase at a time and have the children recite the verse each time. Continue until all words are erased.

- Let the children write verses on heavy paper with large, bold letters. Have them cut the paper apart to make jigsaw puzzles. The children may work their own puzzle or trade puzzles. You might make and duplicate puzzles and then have the children race to work them.

- Let the students throw a ball, beanbag, or stuffed animal to one another. Each student who receives the item must recite a chosen verse or a word from a verse.

- Write verses on strips of paper and cut them in half. Distribute them and tell the students to find the half that matches theirs and then memorize the verse.

- Letter, or have the students letter, verses on index cards. Keep the cards in a box or pocket for the students to study.

- On the board or a transparency show verses that have blanks for key words. Have the class supply the missing words.

- Hold races. Use charts, stickers, stars, and dots to encourage memorizing verses.

- Write Scripture quotations on long cards. Cut them in half and distribute the halves to students. When the first half is read, the student holding the rest of the quotation stands and reads it. For a greater challenge, have the endings read first.

Help the students memorize not by rote, but by heart. Help them make the Scripture words their own. Discuss the meaning of the words and give your students time to think about them and to share what they mean.

Teach memory devices to aid in studying Scripture. For example, here is a jingle to remember the order of the first fourteen New Testament letters (epistles), using the first syllables of each book:

RO-CO-CO,
GAL-EPH-PHI (rhymes with "eye"),
COL-THESS-THESS,
TIM-TIM-TI,
PHIL-HEB. (Think of "Philip.")

Think in groups. Long lists are committed to memory more quickly if they are thought of in categories. For example, the books of the Old Testament are more manageable considered as the Pentateuch, historical books, wisdom books, and prophetic books.

Find helpful associations. I always had trouble remembering who was the murderer and who was the victim in the first homicide until I linked Cain with "cane," a potential weapon.

To remember those books that Catholics accept as divinely inspired and the Protestants do not, think of the Wild West gang J. T. Web and the two McCabes:

J udith
T obit
W isdom
E cclesiaticus
B aruch

and the two McCabes. (1 Maccabees, 2 Maccabees)

Invent acronyms. To teach the three main regions of Palestine in order—Galilee, Samaria, and Judea—make a phrase or sentence with the first letters of each: G, S, J. "Good Saint Joseph" and "God sent Jesus" are possibilities. Likewise, the names and sequence of the books in the Pentateuch (Genesis, Exodus, Leviticus, Numbers, Deuteronomy) can be recalled by nonsense sentences such as this one: Goats eat leaves, not dirt. Or the more helpful code: Jenny has extra levis no doubt (pronounced "deut"). The sillier the device, the easier it is to remember.

Use songs. The following is sung to the alphabet song (A, B, C, D...)

Jesus built his church upon
Peter, Andrew, James, and John,
Simon, Jude, and James the Less,
Philip, Nathanael, and Judas,
Thomas, Matthew, Matthias, too.
My apostles list is through.

CHAPTER 15

Discuss Scripture for Insights

Usually discussion is more fruitful than a monologue. Some principles to keep in mind for discussion are the following:

- State the question or problem clearly and make sure students understand it and know what they are to do.

- Prepare students so that they have the information and the skills needed to carry on an intelligent discussion of the topic.

- Encourage everyone to participate, and discourage anyone from monopolizing the discussion.

- Guide the students to practice courtesy by listening to one another, by expressing themselves politely, and by respecting the opinions of others.

- Keep the students on the topic.

- Summarize the discussion at the end.

Questions for discussion should be chosen carefully. Agree-disagree discussions and debates should not be such that the class arrives at a conclusion that contradicts church teachings. Questions should focus on significant ideas and have meaning for the students. They should be thought-provoking. "Why" questions are more intriguing than who, what, when, and where questions.

Discussions often reveal misconceptions. The catechist should be alert to these and correct them, if not that day, then later.

Discussion can be stimulated by means of a continuum activity. Ask the students a question or give them a statement and let them determine where on a continuum their response would lie. For example:

God does not answer prayers today as they were answered in the Bible.
STRONGLY AGREE   AGREE   DISAGREE   STRONGLY DISAGREE

Responses can be marked on paper. For more concrete involvement, the students can place themselves on an imaginary line stretching across the classroom with its ends representing opposing points of view. After the discussion, students can place themselves on the line again to see which way the class has been swayed.

A Phillips 66 discussion makes a good lead-in to a lesson. Form groups of six. Allow them six minutes to discuss a question such as, "If you were alive when Jesus was and had seen and heard him, what would you think of him?"

Concentric circle discussion motivates students to participate. A group stands inside a circle of students. This inner group discusses while the outer circle listens. Then the students trade places.

Involve the entire class in an open discussion of questions. To save time and to increase confidence, have students prepare the questions ahead of time. Here are sample questions to evoke reflection on the Book of Ruth: Why is Ruth a model of faithful love? What other virtues did she possess? What evidence is there that Boaz was worthy of Ruth? How was Ruth rewarded for her faithfulness? What is God showing us by the fact that Ruth was a Moabite and not Jewish? What people today would particularly profit from reading this book?

The same type of questions that can be discussed in a large group can be discussed in small groups of five, each with its own chairperson. This allows more students to participate actively. Each chairperson gives a group report. Open class discussion follows.

Also with small groups, have an agree-disagree discussion. Compose a set of controversial statements like the following:

- Jesus was more divine than human.
- The early Christian community as described in Acts was not like the church today.
- The stories in the Old Testament have little meaning for us.
- David was a greater Hebrew hero than Moses.

Divide the class into groups of five with a chairperson for each group. Direct the groups to try to come to a definite decision for each statement. Everyone should be encouraged to contribute facts, experiences, and reflective thinking for the consideration of the group. The decision of the majority in each group should be recorded. At the end of the discussion period, allow time for individuals to write summaries. In a forum, compare the results of all the groups and invite comments from the class.

Choose a topic that lends itself to debate such as those suggested for the agree-disagree discussions. Let two teams debate the issue before the class. The debate begins with each side presenting its point of view in a two-minute talk. Then the participants debate. The class can vote to determine which side won.

Hold a panel discussion. Let three to five students form a panel of experts on a certain topic: the Commandments, the Beatitudes, the life of Jesus, the prophets. Have the class write questions on cards or slips of paper. Collect the cards and draw them at random to pose questions to the panel.

A form of discussion called kineposium provides for maximum interaction among students. Its purpose is to generate and share ideas, not to debate. The topics chosen for the kineposium should allow for a diversity of opinions, for example:

- How is the faith God calls us to in Scripture best shown in our lives?
- Which woman in the Old Testament most clearly prefigures Mary?
- Outside of the Resurrection what do you think was Christ's most significant miracle?
- Someone once said that Christianity has not failed, it's just never been tried. Which teaching of Christ seems most difficult for people to "try" today?
- What message from the prophets do we most need today?

Appoint the number of secretaries needed, one for each group. The other students each receive a card listing the group numbers in different orders. (See Illustration N in the Appendix.) At the signal, all go to the first group listed on their cards. After the designated time spent discussing the assigned question, a signal is again given. Everyone then moves to the next group where the secretary checks to make sure everyone is in the right group. (Secretaries do not rotate.) This process is repeated until everyone has been to each group. The secretaries then report. This is followed by a kineposium forum in which anyone may raise questions or make additions.

CHAPTER 16

Write on the Word of God

Creative writing assignments can lead students to delve deeper into the meaning of Scripture and help them to remember it. As students read Scripture, they can record in journals what certain verses mean to them. They can also reply to passages in the form of personal prayers to God written in their journals. More advanced students might write an entire meditation on a Scripture passage.

Have the students write a dialogue between characters, for example, between Samson and his mother after he has been blinded, or between Ezra and Nehemiah as they plan the restoration of Jerusalem, or between Thomas and John as they discuss how Jesus calmed the storm.

Invite the students to write a biblical story from a particular point of view, for example, the sacrifice of Isaac through the eyes of Isaac himself, or Bartimaeus' account of his own cure. Or they can write a story as the "other side" saw it: Satan's report of the Fall, the Egyptian view of the Exodus, the Canaanite account of the Israelite invasion, and Pilate's version of Jesus' trial. One student wrote Goliath's story about the fight with David.

Other writing activities that enable the students to put themselves in the shoes of people in the Bible include the following:

- logs of the Exodus, Jesus' travels, and Paul's missionary journeys
- diary entries of Judas Maccabeus or of an apostle during Holy Week
- prayers that a person in the Bible like Adam, Joseph, Moses, Mary Magdalene, or Dorcas might have prayed

- letters to Adam, Judith, Thomas, or between Jacob and Uncle Laban, Mary and her relative Elizabeth, from great-great-grandmother Eve to us, or from Jesus to us

- speeches that Moses, Isaiah, or Paul might have delivered

- a eulogy for Judith, Samuel, Lazarus, or the Good Thief

- a litany of John the Baptist or of Saint Peter

- text messages between two people: Jonathan and David, God and Moses, Mary and her mother

- a job description for an apostle, a prophet, a builder of the Temple, a carpenter in Nazareth, a soldier in David's army

Writing activities that call for summaries of main ideas include these:

- storyboards for a television show about a biblical event

- a newscast on the battle of Jericho or the Sermon on the Mount

- a telegram describing one of Jesus' miracles in fifteen words or less

- headlines summarizing major happenings in the life of Jesus

- titles for biographies of people in the Bible, for example, Saul's biography might be called "Heart of Darkness," David's "The Loved One," and Solomon's "The Power and the Glory"

- matches of song titles or cars with people: Moses would drive an Odyssey; Daniel, a Chevy Blazer; Peter, a Ford Escape

Writing activities that deepen the students' understanding of biblical themes and require them to synthesize the materials include the following:

- questions for an interview with a person involved in the Exile, or someone who witnessed the raising of the son of the widow of Naim, or someone who was shipwrecked with Paul

- a homily focusing on a biblical theme for a Sunday Mass (one student of mine actually had her parish priest deliver the homily she wrote on the Good Shepherd—to the delight of the parishioners)

- a sixty-second reflection that could be given in a dial-a-message telephone program

- a commercial related to a Bible story

- all forms of poems on biblical subjects (See samples in Illustration O in the Appendix.)

- an edition of a newspaper (*The Israeli Daily*, *The Jerusalem Journal*) centered on a major event in salvation history like the flood, the Exodus, the Exile, the return to Jerusalem, the raising of Lazarus, the crucifixion, or the Resurrection.

  One of my students composed an edition of the *Desert Herald*. The front page article described Moses striking the rock twice. Articles included a weather report (a sandstorm), a traffic death (a pedestrian mysteriously struck down by a hit-and-run camel), obituaries (the pedestrian left behind seven wives, twenty children, six sheep, and two tents), and an advertisement (this page brought to you by Berstein and Berstein, best used camels in the desert). The editorial chided the Israelites for complaining to God. A unique feature was this lament on the recipe page: "Mom, we are sick and tired of having quail and manna for breakfast, lunch, and dinner! When are we going to eat regular food again?" It was followed by creative ways to serve manna and quail for each of the three meals. After reading that, few people would forget what the Israelites ate in the desert!

- a website for a biblical person or the Temple, the town of Bethlehem, Jerusalem, the early church

- a Wikipedia entry for a biblical person, place, or event

CHAPTER 17

Pray Using the Scriptures

In an article in the September 27, 1986, issue of *America*, the late Archbishop John F. Whealon of Hartford, Connecticut, challenged us to be "a Bible-reading, Bible-loving, Bible-quoting, Bible-living Catholic people" in order to confront the threat of fundamentalism. We can be this if we are a Bible-praying people. The Bible, the meeting place of God and God's people, not only prompts us to pray, but is replete with ready-made prayers. *The Bible Prayer Book* by Eugene S. Geissler (Ave Maria Press), which is a collection of all the prayers, songs, hymns, and blessings in the Bible, is 528 pages long!

Teach your students to pray Scripture. Encourage them to adopt some of the gems in the Bible as their own, such as Psalms 23, 51, and 139, or Habakkuk's brilliant act of faith:

> For though the fig tree blossom not
> nor fruit be on the vines.
> Though the yield of the olive fail
> and the terraces produce no nourishment,
> Though the flocks disappear from the fold
> and there be no herd in the stalls,
> Yet will I rejoice in the Lord
> and exult in my saving God.
> HABAKKUK 3:17–18

Write short prayers on the board taken from different books of the Bible and use them before, during, or after class. Point out how one-liners like these in the Bible often make good prayers:

> "Lord, I believe. Help my unbelief" (the possessed boy's father).

"Speak, Lord. Your servant is listening" (Samuel).

"Lord, to whom shall we go? You have the words of eternal life" (Peter).

"My Lord and my God" (Thomas).

Play songs that are musical arrangements of Scripture or reflections on Scripture verses. Invite the students to turn the songs into prayers by meditating on the words.

Use sections of the Bible for prayer activities in a lesson. Ask students to formulate petitions based on the Beatitudes, the Commandments, or the works of mercy. Intersperse short readings from John's account of Jesus' last discourse with time for reflection.

Encourage students to pray Scripture verses aloud. The more the body is involved by voicing and hearing the words, the more effective the prayer is.

Pray parts of Psalm 136 and then invite the students to add lines that merit the response **"His love is everlasting."** It should end up something like this:

> Give thanks to Yahweh, for he is good,
> *his love is everlasting!*
>
> He alone performs great marvels,
> *his love is everlasting!*
>
> His wisdom made the heavens,
> *his love is everlasting!*
>
> He led his people through the wilderness,
> *his love is everlasting!*
>
> He remembered us when we were down,
> *his love is everlasting!*
>
> He brought my lost puppy back,
> *his love is everlasting!*
>
> He gave us beautiful weather today,
> *his love is everlasting!*
>
> He helped me pass a math test,
> *his love is everlasting!*
> —Adapted from Psalm 136, *Jerusalem Bible*

A similar prayer can be made based on Daniel 3:57–90. This time the students list created things and people in their lives and then respond with the prayer **"Praise and exalt him above all forever."**

> Bless the Lord, all you works of the Lord,…
>
> Angels of the Lord, bless the Lord,…
>
> You heavens, bless the Lord,…
>
> Sun and moon, bless the Lord,…

Have the students sit quietly and page through a gospel from beginning to end, letting the headings bring to mind the events in Christ's life. Encourage them to reflect quietly on this overview in the presence of Jesus.

Introduce the scriptural rosary. Before each Hail Mary, read a passage or a line from Scripture about the decade's mystery:

For the **Joyful Mysteries**, these would be appropriate:
Annunciation: Luke 1:26–38
Visitation: Luke 1:39–56
Birth of Jesus: Luke 2:1–20; Philippians 2:6, 7
Presentation: Luke 2:22–32
Finding of Jesus in the Temple: Luke 2:41–50

For the **Luminous Mysteries**, use these:
Baptism: Matthew 3:14–17
Wedding at Cana: John 2:1–4
Proclamation of the kingdom: Mark 1:15
Transfiguration: Luke 9:28–36
Institution of the Eucharist: Matthew 26:26–28

For the **Sorrowful Mysteries**, use these verses:
Agony in the Garden: Matthew 26:36–46
Scourging: Matthew 26:67; 27:20–26
Crowning with Thorns: Matthew 27:27–30; Philippians 2:8–11
Carrying of the Cross: John 19:12–17
Crucifixion: Matthew 27:45–54

For the **Glorious Mysteries**, use the following:

    Resurrection: Matthew 28:1–10; Mark 16:2–7

    Ascension: Matthew 28:11–20; Acts 1:10, 11

    Descent of the Holy Spirit: Acts 2:1–11; 41, 42

    Assumption: Luke 1:41–50

    Crowning of Mary as Queen of Heaven: Revelation 12:1–2

As a variation, substitute other events in Christ's life for the traditional twenty mysteries. For example, the students might pray the Parable Mysteries or the Miracle Mysteries.

Teach students to meditate using the following method:

Still the body: Have them still their mouths, hands, and feet. Ask older students to refrain from jiggling their feet nervously. Tell younger ones to have listening hands and feet. Have them close their eyes. Adolescents will feel freer if you stand in the back of the room. Enter into the meditation with the class, but don't close *your* eyes.

Quiet the mind: Tell them to focus on God, present here, loving them, waiting to speak to them.

Read the Scripture passage.

Recreate the story in the imagination: Guide them through it again, suggesting insights, offering descriptions.

Reflect on the story: Make it personal. Be a facilitator. Ask questions.

Respond to the Scripture: Let this take the form of a resolution or prayer. Lead the students into this by questions. Suggest topics of conversation. (See the sample meditation based on the story of Zacchaeus in Illustration P in the Appendix.)

These Scripture stories are good for meditation:

    The boy Jesus in the Temple (Luke 2:41–50)

    Temptation in the desert (Matthew 4:1–11)

    Calling the first disciples (Matthew 4:18–22)

    Calming the storm (Luke 8:22–25)

    Healing of a leper (Luke 5:12–16)

    Healing of a paralyzed man (Luke 5:17–26)

    Jesus and the sinful woman (Luke 7:36–50)

Blessing the children (Luke 18:15–17)

Healing a blind beggar (Luke 18:35–43)

Miracle of the loaves (John 6:1–13)

Jesus and Zacchaeus (Luke 19:1–10)

The widow's offering (Luke 21:1–4)

The rich young man (Matthew 19:16–22)

The raising of Lazarus (John 11:1–44)

Driving out the moneychangers (Mark 11:15–17)

The Last Supper (Luke 22:14–23)

Washing the disciples' feet (John 13:1–11)

Agony in the garden (Luke 22:39–46)

The Crucifixion (Luke 23:33–49)

On the way to Emmaus (Luke 24:13–35)

The prophet Ezekiel ate the scroll containing the words of the Lord. He said, "It was as sweet as honey in my mouth" (Ezekiel 3:3). We are to savor the words of Scripture just as we savor a piece of Werther's candy. One way to do this is to pray a mantra, a short prayer repeated over and over. Psalm verses especially make good mantras:

You are my Lord; I have no good apart from you. PSALM 16:2

I love you, O Lord, my strength. PSALM 18:1

Do not be far from me, for trouble is near. PSALM 22:11

Let your steadfast love, O Lord, be upon us. PSALM 33:22

O God, you are my God, I seek you. PSALM 63:1

How great are your works, O Lord! PSALM 92:5

I give you thanks, O Lord, with my whole heart. PSALM 138:1

Some Scripture verses may be used as "reverse mantras." That is, we repeat God's words to us:

I, the Lord your God, hold your right hand. ISAIAH 41:13

I have called you by name, you are mine. ISAIAH 43:1

Do not be afraid. MATTHEW 14:27

I am with you always. MATTHEW 28:20

Some psalms are alphabetic; each verse begins with a letter of the Hebrew alphabet. Have your students write prayer acrostics using their names. For example, Erin wrote:

E   njoy the Lord!

R   ejoice in his name.

I   n the Lord is our salvation.

N   ever forget who he is.

Teach the students to pray the psalms in different ways:

- Alternate sides in praying the verses.

- Have a reader pray the entire psalm with all responding to each verse with an antiphon.

- Pray the psalm together, have a few moments of silence, and then have individuals add to it by

  repeating a line that is particularly meaningful to them,

  paraphrasing a verse, or

  repeating a verse and adding to it.

Here is an example for the praying of Psalm 23:1–4 this last way:

All   The Lord is my shepherd; I shall not want. In verdant pastures he gives me repose; Beside restful waters he leads me; he refreshes my soul. He guides me in right paths for his name's sake. Even though I walk in the dark valley I fear no evil; for you are at my side with your rod and your staff that give me courage.

Student 1   He refreshes my soul.

Student 2   You are at my side.

Student 3   He guides me in making right decisions.

Student 4   I shall not want anything. I'll have all the peace and love I need.

Student 5   I fear no evil, not even when people try to ruin my reputation.

This method works well with Psalms 1, 8, 54, 91, 93, 100, 116, 121, 130, or 138.

Have the students pray while creating a piece of art. Give them each a piece of aluminum foil and explain that they will experience a prayer-in-action. Ask the students what their favorite gospel story is—would it be a miracle, a teaching of Jesus, or an event in Jesus' life? Then have them think of a symbol that would represent this story. Direct the students to make this symbol out of the aluminum foil silently and prayerfully. They should think about what the story means to them and speak to Jesus about it. When the students are finished, have them turn to another person or two and tell about their symbol and why they chose it. This activity is equally effective with pipe cleaners, paper to be torn, or clay (pray dough!).

Be creative in using Scripture for prayer. One of our high schools was chosen a National School of Excellence. At the public celebration the principal led everyone in a closing litany based on the story of creation. She spoke sentences about the work and the contribution of people that had made the award possible. After each sentence, the auditorium full of people responded "That's good!" For instance, "Forty-two dedicated teachers come to school each day.... That's good!" The total effect was delightful and very moving.

A marvelous way to sound the depths of Scripture is *lectio divina* (sacred reading). It is hearing God speak to you through one passage. You let the word of God happen in you. Meister Eckhart said, "God is always at home, it is we who have gone out for a walk." In *lectio divina*, we come home.

Lectio divina has its origins in monasteries long ago. Monks gathered in a room where one of them read aloud from the Bible. They listened and when a passage appealed to them, they left, taking away that word with them to pray over.

To begin this prayer, you become aware of God's presence. Realize that God is looking at you, loving you. Then there are four steps, which have been compared to four rungs on Jacob's ladder (in Genesis, Jacob saw a ladder that led to paradise).

> **1. Lectio (reading).** You read the passage slowly. The purpose of this reading is not to stimulate your mind to curiosity, but to awaken your heart to prayer. Let a word or phrase touch you. It will stand out, and your mind will focus on it. Repeat the words and let them sink into your heart and mind, to become part of you. Savor, relish, enjoy the word. Let it saturate you, form your heart. In this step you put the reading into your mouth as a grape in the winepress. You might want to know why a particular verse has attracted your attention and what it might mean for you. This moves you into the next step.

> **2. Meditatio (meditating).** You wrestle with the word, probe it, ponder it, seek its meaning for your life and your unique relationship with God. This step is like pressing the grape, drawing the juice that will ferment into wine. Your heart presses the word. Remember that vintage wine takes time. At some point you will realize the word means something to you. This is the "aha moment." You are moved deeply by God's word. You experience profound feelings and are ready to respond, to enter the third step.

3. Oratio (praying). Prayer moves from mind to heart. You let the word or phrase touch your heart. You talk to God about it. Let your heart speak, sing, celebrate, cry. What response does the word call forth from you—praise? thanksgiving? sorrow? peace? Stay with those feelings. Don't try to understand them. Just stay in loving silence. Make an effort to put yourself at the disposal of God's Spirit, preparing for God's action. You should focus on God. This leads into the final step.

4. Contemplatio (contemplating). This is "a simple loving gaze." Be alone with God in the great silence that is too deep for words. Here God takes over your faculties and takes the lead. You have a direct experience of God. Listen to what God says to you about the word. The goal of *lectio divina* is this last step, union with God, when it may seem as if nothing is happening. A piece of Zen wisdom sheds light on this step: "Sitting still, doing nothing, Spring comes, and the grass grows by itself."

These steps can occur in any order and take any length of time. You may repeat steps several times or just do one. When you are distracted or can't sustain the prayer, read the passage again until another word strikes you. Notice that the first three steps involve doing. The last step is simply being. The four steps move from words to wordlessness.

Someone has renamed the steps the four movements: receiving, appropriating, responding, union. John of the Cross outlined the four steps this way:

Seek in READING

and you will find in MEDITATION.

Knock in PRAYER

and it will be opened to you in CONTEMPLATION.

Dom Marmion paraphrased the steps even more simply:

We read

under the eye of God

until the heart is touched

and leaps to flame.

Introduce the students to *lectio divina* and have them experience it. Light a candle to recall God's presence. Form groups of four or five. In each group one person reads a passage while all listen. Then another person reads the passage. Allow time for a word or phrase to touch the students' hearts. Then they reflect aloud. (Reflecting differs from discussion.) Some may simply share a word that has meaning for them. Have them listen to a related song. Then invite them to make a prayer response aloud—one sentence that their word prompts them to pray: thanksgiving, petition, adoration, love, or sorrow. Let the students sit in silence for a time.

CHAPTER 18

Simulate Biblical Events

To give the students a feeling for how some of the books of the Bible were written, let them pretend to be inspired writers today. Have them select an audience and a message it needs to hear. Help them decide on a form. Then let them write the message and deliver it.

Maybe you've seen the Holy Land mapped out in Chautauqua, New York, on the shore of Lake Chautauqua. In a similar manner, you can have your class create Palestine on the playground with chalk and then play out events like the Exodus and the Exile.

A SEDER MEAL

Your students could hold a Seder meal. The meaning of Passover will be more firmly entrenched in their minds, and they will have a better understanding of the Jewish people. Perhaps you can invite a Jewish person or a Rabbi to assist with your Seder meal. (The complete English service with directions is in the booklet *Haggadah for the American Family*, published by Haggadah Institute, 15001 SW 153 Place, Miami, Florida, 33196; www.americanhaggadah.com.)

Secure volunteers to provide matzoh, salt, parsley or lettuce, horseradish, charoses (a mixture of chopped apple, nuts, and cinnamon moistened with wine), grape juice, plates, and dishes. Candles and flowers will make the table more festive.

You might wish to prepare the special Seder plate of symbolic foods: bitter herbs (horseradish), a vegetable (parsley or lettuce), a more bitter vegetable (radish), charoses, a bone, and a hard-boiled egg. Inform the students that the egg is a symbol of the sacrifices offered at the Temple. The other foods are explained during the service itself.

Before the Passover meal, tell the students that they will drink from the cup four times because of the fourfold promise the Lord made to the Israelites: "I will bring you forth," "I will deliver you," "I will redeem you," and "I will take you." Also explain that the extra cup of wine on the table is for Elijah the prophet, who is to announce the day of universal peace and love on his return. (See Illustration Q in the Appendix for an adaptation of the Seder meal ritual.)

Make **matzoh**, unleavened bread:
    3½ cups flour (if whole wheat, 1 cup)
    1 cup water
    2 tsp salt

    Mix ingredients. Divide dough into four parts. Roll out each part as thin as possible into 6-inch squares. Prick the surface with fork and bake at 400° until golden brown, twelve to fifteen minutes. Serve with a dip or spread.

Recipe for **charoses**
    6 apples (peeled, cored, and diced)
    1 cup walnuts or pecans, chopped
    ⅓ cup sweet red wine
    ½ tsp cinnamon
    1 tsp white sugar
    3½ tsp honey

CHAPTER 19

Collect Bible-Related Materials

If you have avid collectors of baseball cards, stickers, coins, and stamps, transform them into collectors of biblical items. Throughout your Scripture studies, encourage your students to watch for newspaper and magazine articles on the Bible. These can be shared with the class and then posted. Have the students be on the lookout for references to the Bible on TV, over the radio, on billboards, or in books. They can record these references in their notebooks and then report them to the class.

Have the students make scrapbooks: a scrapbook about Israel complete with illustrations, or a scrapbook on a particular book of the Bible. As an alternative, let students collect objects in a shoe box. A Genesis shoe box might contain such things as an article on how the universe began, a plastic apple, a button that says, "I belong to God," a rainbow magnet, a poem about Abraham, an English-French pocket dictionary, and a picture of a pyramid.

As a culminating project, students could assemble a booklet of their favorite passages in the Bible interspersed with pictures and drawings. Another possibility is to have them make a prayerbook of biblical prayers. They might enjoy making a tiny book.

As an ongoing activity, students could collect biblical terms and produce a dictionary. They can illustrate the entries to make a picture dictionary. This last can be a class project with each student volunteering to do one or more pages.

Have your students go on a scavenger hunt looking for things that play a role in Scripture, such as dice, a penny, seeds. When the students bring back the items, discuss them.

CHAPTER 20

Use Programmed Learning for Efficient Learning

Granted the goal of biblical study is not so much information as transformation, yet there is a definite body of knowledge we want students to master. The best way I know to teach many facts and concepts fast and well is programmed learning, a form of independent study. There are arguments against it; the strongest argument for it is that it works.

In programmed learning, concepts are presented in frames that the students read by themselves, using a cover sheet and revealing one frame at a time. As they progress through the lesson acquiring new bits of knowledge, they meet questions about information from previous frames. The answer to each question appears in the next frame for immediate feedback. The frames can be set in two columns so that the students fold the sheet in half and go down one column at a time.

This method is good for variety, and the students like it, especially if it is introduced as a chance for them to teach themselves. Tests given shortly after usually yield high scores and give the students personal satisfaction. Doing programmed learning individually allows students to go at their own pace. However, by projecting the frames on a screen you can carry it out as a whole-class activity. A student or group of students might be challenged to create a programmed learning activity on a book of the Bible or a Bible story for the rest of the class.

Background information on the Bible is one topic that can easily be taught by programmed learning. Here is an example:

"Bible" comes from a Greek word for book.

The Bible is a collection of books written between 1400 B.C. and 100 A.D. The primary author of the Bible is God, so the Bible is sacred.

There are two main divisions in the Bible. The Old Testament is written mostly in Hebrew and contains forty-six books. **What does "Bible" mean?**

BOOK

The New Testament was written mainly in Greek and contains twenty-seven books. **Who is the primary author of the Bible?**

GOD

The church determined which books belong to the Bible. Catholics accept more books in the Old Testament than the Jewish people and Protestants. **How many books are in the Old Testament?**

FORTY-SIX

The Old Testament tells the history of Israel, God's chosen people. **Who determined what books belong to the Bible?**

THE CHURCH

The New Testament tells the story of Christ and his church. **How many books are in the New Testament?**

TWENTY-SEVEN

We say that God inspired the Bible. This means that God directed the minds and wills of the human authors to write what God wished to reveal. **Which part of the Bible tells the history of Israel?**

OLD TESTAMENT

The Bible is also called Sacred Scripture. "Scripture" means writings. The Bible contains many forms of writing such as letters, poetry, short stories, and prayers. **Why is God the primary author of the Bible?**

GOD INSPIRED IT

In order to understand a book of the Bible, it helps to know its form. Davy Crockett, the frontiersman, really existed, but his killing a bear when he was three years old is part of a legend about him. Similarly, some biblical stories are not meant to be taken literally. **What does the New Testament tell about?**

CHRIST AND THE CHURCH

The Bible is not meant to teach historical or scientific truth. Its truth lies in what it reveals about God and our relationship with God. **What does it mean to say that God inspired the Bible?**

GOD DIRECTS THE MINDS AND WILLS OF THE HUMAN AUTHORS TO WRITE WHAT GOD WISHED TO REVEAL

The church, the believing community, has the power to interpret the Bible correctly. **Must everything in the Bible be understood as fact?**

NO

Who interprets the Bible correctly?

THE CHURCH

CHAPTER 21

Play Bible Games

Scripture scholar Raymond Brown once said, "The Scriptures are a plaything which the Father gives us to enjoy." Lead children into Scripture through play. Be alert for biblical crossword puzzles and word searches. (See Illustrations A and R in the Appendix.) Invent your own puzzles and games, such as board games and mazes, and have your students invent them. Invest in books, publications, or computer software that contain ideas for making Scripture study fun. The company Creative Teaching offers several Bible-based games for all grade levels (54732 Shelby Road, Suite #231, Shelby Township, MI 48316; www.creativeteaching.net). In addition a wealth of free material can be found by typing "Bible activity sheets" in a search engine. You can also find templates for PowerPoint games on the Internet. Remember that games are much more enjoyable for children when prizes are awarded. Prizes also spur them on to do their best.

To lighten review lessons, cut up pictures of biblical stories and have the children piece the puzzle together and identify the story. You might paste the pictures on foam plates first. With older students pin names of biblical persons on the backs of individuals and have them ask their classmates yes and no questions until they figure out who they are. Challenge the class with riddles, maybe in the form of poems. Have your students play charades, Pictionary, baseball, tic-tac-toe, Hangman, Truth or Lie, Snakes and Ladders, and Jeopardy, using Scripture concepts.

To review biblical terms, play "Vocab." Have the students set up their papers like Bingo cards with V-O-C-A-B across the top and a free space in the middle. Instruct them to write a term or name from the unit to be reviewed in each block. Prepare a set of cards with the same terms. Distribute markers to each student. As each term is drawn from the cards, a student must identify it. Students who have that term on their cards cover it with a marker. The game proceeds until someone has "Vocab."

Here are some possible terms for a bingo game on Israel's kings:

Samuel	anoint	Jonathan	wisdom	Jerusalem
Saul	Goliath	Philistine	Bethlehem	shepherd
David	temple	Absalom	Israel	Ark of the Covenant
Solomon	psalms	Nathan	Abner	obedience
monarchy	proverbs	Bathsheba	Jesse	

To provide practice in looking up Scripture references, hold a contest. Distribute a sheet of ten questions with the Scripture references that contain the answer to each. Make the questions interesting, for example:

1. Who made clothes for Adam and Eve? (Genesis 3:21)

2. How old was Moses when he asked Pharaoh to let the Israelites go? (Exodus 7:7)

3. What kind of person says there is no God? (Psalms 53:1)

4. What is a lovely woman who is rebellious like? (Proverbs 11:22)

5. What animals did David kill single-handedly? (1 Samuel 17:36)

6. What did Amos call the wealthy ladies of Israel? (Amos 4:1)

7. What did Jesus say we must make our home? (John 8:31)

8. Who let Peter out of prison? (Acts 12:7)

9. How many times was Paul whipped for being a Christian? (2 Corinthians 11:24)

10. What does the Bible ask Jesus to do at its close? (Revelation 22:20)

The first one to find the answers to all ten questions wins. In case you're wondering, here are the answers: 1 = Yahweh; 2 = eighty; 3 = a fool; 4 = a golden ring in the snout of a pig; 5 = a lion and a bear; 6 = cows; 7 = his word; 8 = an angel; 9 = 195 (5 times 39); 10 = come

To involve your whole school or religious education program in biblical games, plan a Bible Bazaar with your students. Let them brainstorm to organize booths and activities related to the Bible. Money collected can be donated to an organization that works for social justice to fulfill the injunctions of biblical prophets like Amos. Prizes for any of the games could be biblical, e.g., a Bible, a cake decorated like a Bible, a CD of biblical songs. You might use some of these starter ideas for your Bible Bazaar activities:

- A word search for the participants as they enter (See Illustration A in the Appendix.)

- A booth where stones, buttons, and plaques with Scripture quotations lettered on them are sold

- The presentation of a short play about a biblical story

- A Jacob's Well fishpond where Jonah's whales are caught

- Instant Bingo in which players draw folded papers containing Scripture references and then look them up to see if they match any of the winning verses that are posted

- A Wise Man's booth where a correct answer to a question on the Bible entitles the player to a chance at a large prize

- A penny pitch game in which players toss pennies, trying to land on the "promised land"

- A Spread-the-Word booth for attaching Scripture messages to helium balloons and releasing them into the sky

A variation of a crossword puzzle is a switchboard puzzle. The squares are already filled in, and the students must supply the clues.

In connection with studying the Old Testament, students might make a dreidel and play the Jewish Passover game with it. On a four-inch square of tagboard they write the Hebrew letters for N, G, H, and S, one along each side. A pencil or other stick is inserted in the center of the tagboard as a spinner. (For a smaller dreidel a toothpick can be used.) Each player puts some tokens (chips, beans, raisins, nuts, or pennies) into the pot. The students take turns spinning the dreidel and, when it falls on its side, doing as the Hebrew letter at the top directs. (See the code below.) The player who has the most tokens wins.

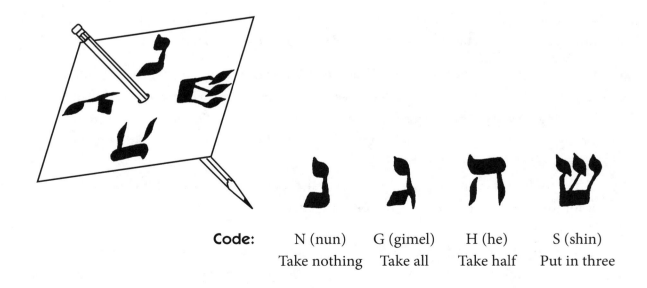

Code:	N (nun)	G (gimel)	H (he)	S (shin)
	Take nothing	Take all	Take half	Put in three

CHAPTER 22

Set Up Learning Stations with Scripture Activities

A teaching technique that students find exciting is learning stations. For a topic to be studied, think of five or six short and varied activities. Set up a station in the room for each activity. Mark it with a large number and supply it with directions and materials needed to carry out the activity. Explain to the students the general idea of each activity and give them each a card indicating the order in which they are to move from station to station. At definite time intervals, give a signal for the students to move to their next station.

Here is a set of activities for learning stations on the Book of Psalms:

STATION 1: The students study information on the psalms from a sheet of paper. When they are ready, one of them dictates an oral quiz from a card in an envelope.

> The psalms are the song-prayers of Israel collected over a period of 700 years. Some of the 150 psalms are believed to have been written by King David, who was skilled at playing the harp. The Psalms are collected in a book of the Bible situated approximately in the middle of the Bible. As God's inspired word, they are a living source of power.
>
> The psalms have many purposes. They praise and thank God, ask for God's help or forgiveness, and ask for blessings on the leaders of the land. Some are even complaints to God.
>
> Some psalms remind people of how God acted to save them, and some encourage them to follow God's law. Certain verses of the "messianic psalms" can be interpreted to apply to Jesus.

The psalms were the official prayer of Israel used in the Temple service. They were the prayers of Jesus and Mary. Today, the psalms are still popular prayers. Psalm 8 is the "moon psalm" quoted in connection with the Apollo 8 flight. We pray and sing the psalms at Mass. Every day priests, religious, and other Christians pray the Liturgy of the Hours, which is composed mainly of psalms. Many people like to pray the psalms as personal prayer. Perhaps you, too, will learn to love and pray the psalms.

Quiz

1. What are psalms?

2. How many are there?

3. Who wrote some of them?

4. What are the purposes of the psalms?

STATION 2: The students pray psalms in three different ways:

A leader recites Psalm 46, with the rest saying the last two repeating lines of each stanza.

The group divides into two and recites Psalm 98, alternating verses.

The entire group prays Psalm 150 together.

STATION 3: The students listen to a psalm set to music while viewing related pictures.

STATION 4: The students design a bookmark from a psalm verse, choosing from this list:

My God, my rock of refuge (Psalm 18:3).

The heavens declare the glory of God (Psalm 19:2).

Beside restful waters God leads me (Psalm 23:2).

God guides me in right paths (Psalm 23:3).

Be glad in the Lord and rejoice, you just (Psalm 32:11).

God made firm my steps (Psalm 40:3).

My joy lies in being close to God (Psalm 73:28, *Jerusalem Bible*).

You are the God who works wonders (Psalm 77:15).

Your love for me has been so great (Psalm 86:13, *Jerusalem Bible*).

I mean to sing to Yahweh all my life (Psalm 104:33, *Jerusalem Bible*).

God's love is everlasting (Psalm 107:1, *Jerusalem Bible*).

STATION 5: The students write their own psalms using as a model Psalm 5, 8, 23, 136, or another short psalm. (See Chapter 8, "Rewrite Scripture," page 28.)

STATION 6: The students match psalm verses with human feelings.

When I am frightened because people are attacking me…

When I am worried…

When I am at peace…

When I am in awe at God's power…

When I feel guilty…

When I am grateful to God…

When I am happy because of God's love for me…

A. Psalm 23
B. Psalm 69:14–17
C. Psalm 138
D. Psalm 47:1–7
E. Psalm 131
F. Psalm 51:1–11
G. Psalm 145

Answers may vary: B, A, E, G, F, C, D

Other topics that can be taught by means of learning stations are the Exodus, wisdom books, the prophets, Jesus' miracles, Jesus' teachings, and the New Testament letters.

CHAPTER 23

Use
Audiovisuals

Today there are many fine audiovisuals with biblical themes on the market. Students will enjoy movies such as *The Bible*, *Jacob and Joseph*, *Jesus of Nazareth*, *Jesus Christ Superstar*, and *Godspell*. Most of these are available as DVDs and videocassettes. Visit your school and diocesan libraries as well as the public library for these and other Bible-based movies.

Perhaps you're one of those people who hesitate to use technology of any kind. If this is the case, find someone else to operate the equipment for you, but don't deprive your students of audiovisuals. With a preview and a follow-up discussion or activity, an AV program can be a memorable learning experience. DVDs, videos, filmstrips, and other commercially produced programs are most worthwhile when they are chosen with care to fit the lesson. Don't just use them as a last resort because your lesson isn't planned!

Take advantage of biblical movies and programs on television by calling the students' attention to them. To motivate the students to watch these, offer extra credit for a brief report.

Use a digital camera. Teach lessons using photos you've taken. Take pictures of the students, their work, and performances and display them—with their parents' permission.

Have your students make audiovisual aids like the following:

- Figures for the flannelboard made out of flannel or from paper with a piece of flannel glued to the back

- A scroll of pictures for the opaque projector using student drawings, magazine pictures, or both

- A recording of a biblical passage with background music and an introduction

- A PowerPoint presentation using photos taken with a digital camera of clay, paper, or drawn representations of scenes from a biblical story (See Illustration S in the Appendix for pictures about Jonah.)
- A homemade video using video equipment or a digital camera that takes movies
- Transparencies or cutout figures for an overhead presentation

NOTE: Although cell phones are usually a distraction in class, a creative teacher will find ways to incorporate them in lessons and use their features.

Students can present a demonstration of creation on the overhead in this manner:

1. The program opens with a Pyrex dish filled with water on the overhead and a cutout dove (the Spirit) above it.

2. The water is blown from the side to represent the mighty wind that swept over the water.

3. An Alka-Seltzer is dropped into the water to give the impression of creative action.

4. A sheet of paper masks one half of the screen on a diagonal to show the division of light and darkness.

5. Drops of blue food coloring in the bottom of the dish represent the division of water.

6. Transparencies show the rest of the days of creation. These are made by cutting away forms from paper and then backing the figures that remain in the sheet with pieces of colored cellophane. (See Illustration T in the Appendix.)

As a background to this, one of my classes used a recording of Charlton Heston reading the creation account from Genesis. At the times when the reading was broken by a song, a cut glass bowl was rotated above the overhead, casting lovely designs of light on the screen.

Any concrete object related to a topic can reinforce a lesson. For example, a sand dollar can be a lead-in to a lesson on the Crucifixion. For a dramatic introduction to Jeremiah who prophesied through symbolic actions, shatter an inexpensive earthenware jar in front of the class—far enough away so that no one is hurt. Bring a packet of seeds to class when teaching about the sower or the mustard seed. Tell the story of Jesus' final days on earth using objects such as palm branches, bread, and dice.

Have a group of students prepare a slide meditation or PowerPoint presentation with music to accompany Scripture passages that are centered on a theme such as faith, hope, or God's love.

Challenge the students to assemble a multimedia presentation as a culminating activity. They can combine live or recorded music, slides and photos (perhaps from their own homes), and transparencies in any number of ways to create a powerful lesson.

Remember to make use of the oldest classroom audiovisual: the chalkboard! Write key words and concepts on it, draw on it, and have the students use it too.

See the next chapter for ideas using computers.

CHAPTER 24

Computerize Bible Lessons

To put some wine into new wineskins, so to speak, make use of the computer to teach biblical concepts. Various Bible translations, commentaries, Bible reference works, the sites of the Holy Land, maps, and biblical art, games, Bible stories, and quizzes are now all on CD-ROM. Programs are multiplying by the minute.

Use the interactive whiteboard (if your room has one) to teach biblical material and play review games.

Introduce your students to Catholic websites related to Scripture such as www.sacredspace.ie.

You (and your students) can create exciting electronic slide presentations that combine text and graphics. These can include transition effects, moving-typeface-style animation, digital movies, and sound effects. The slides may be presented on a television using a computer-to-TV adapter. For very large groups, you would need an LCD panel or projector. Dozens of software programs are available to create these multimedia presentations, such as Microsoft's PowerPoint.

You might try creating your own computer programs to teach, review, and test material on the Bible. A word of caution: avoid programs that spend much more time on games than on actual tasks. Also, if there's no obvious faith message in a computer game or program, it isn't worth it. A final warning: do not let fascination with technology cause you to overdo it in your classroom. It makes more of an impact when used sparingly.

CHAPTER 25

Celebrate Sacred Scripture

One day I met a convert of a year and a half. She was an attractive woman with three teen-aged children. She had shopped around for a religion and had decided on Catholicism. She explained, "I chose to be a Catholic because of the way they celebrate the word."

The rituals, gestures, songs, and prayers of a celebration sink deep down into the heart of a child. Celebrations make us realize profound realities. They form convictions and shape attitudes. It is important to celebrate the word with our students.

One ideal time for a celebration of the Bible is National Bible Week, which is observed annually from the Sunday before Thanksgiving to the Sunday after Thanksgiving. Make refreshments part of your celebration. For instance, provide a Star of David cake for an Old Testament celebration.

Catechists concerned about covering content might feel guilty taking time for such a celebration. They should think of it, however, as a lesson on liturgy. For, as Romano Guardini said, "The liturgy does not wish to achieve anything, but merely wants to dwell in the presence of God, to breathe and unfold, to love and praise him." The *Constitution on the Sacred Liturgy* encourages celebrations that help the children to understand some of the elements of the liturgy. It states: "Such celebrations can do much to enhance their appreciation of the word of God" (14).

If students receive personal copies of the Bible for use during the year, why not present them in a special ceremony? Possibly a priest or other guest could give a talk on Scripture, bless the Bibles, and then distribute them. The distribution makes more of an impact if each student is called by name, presented with the Bible, and exhorted to hear God's word and keep it. Appropriate prayers, readings, and songs can be chosen to enrich the celebration.

In other celebrations, honor the Bible by carrying it in procession, holding it high, and enthroning it. The sacredness of the Bible is conveyed to the children when we handle it with reverence and carry out rituals such as bowing to the Bible, kissing it, and burning incense.

The classroom Bible can be kept open on a stand throughout the year. Flowers and candles can be placed near it as symbols of the life and light the word of God is for us.

Occasionally younger children can be invited to clap or cheer after a reading from Scripture.

A good culminating activity for a unit is a prayer service that incorporates Scripture readings and time for reflection on the word. The students can help plan it. (See Illustration U in the Appendix for a prayer service on the word of God itself. Its simple format can be followed for other topics.)

CHAPTER 26

Apply God's Word to Life

Blessed are those who hear the word of God and keep it. This was what Jesus proclaimed. We must teach the students that reading Scripture isn't enough. We need to question: How am I living the words? What is God saying to me? What is my response? Then the word of God will be planted in our hearts and bear fruit.

We can't give students what we don't have. We must encounter God's word working in our hearts if we wish to touch the lives of our children. The best way to lead students to a love and knowledge of Scripture is to assign it an important role in our own lives. Reading the Bible, praying it, and reflecting over it, we come to value it. Only then are we able to communicate that sense of value to those we teach.

If we believe that God speaks to us today through Scripture, we will read it from the perspective of our own situations. We will draw parallels with our own lives and be nourished by the word. The following is a reflection on the Book of Jonah as seen through the eyes of a catechist. It is an attempt to relate Scripture to our very real and present situations.

JONAH, PATRON OF CATECHISTS

For too long the prophet Jonah has been overshadowed (or swallowed up?) by the great fish that swam into his life. Granted, this fish with the cast-iron stomach is an important supporting character in the tale. But when measured by instruments other than yardsticks, a person is bigger than a fish.

Anyone not distracted by the whale will realize that Jonah is a prime candidate for the role of patron of catechists. He is no superhero like Abraham, Moses, or David. He does not stride across the pages of the Bible in sandals too large for the average Christian to wear. He does not possess a secret weapon (like Samson's hair). Nor does he have to withstand a hundred and one forms of persecution as Jeremiah did. All in all, Jonah is an ordinary man living an ordinary prophet's life.

Jonah, utterly and pitifully human in his faults and foibles, goes about his noble task of prophesying, showing fear, anger, obstinacy, and unpredictability. And yet, God uses him to accomplish the impossible. Because of Jonah's flawed but successful service, he offers hope to every aspiring catechist who is less than perfect.

The story of Jonah opens with God's command to him to march into Nineveh, the capital of Israel's dreaded enemy Assyria. His mission: to preach against Nineveh and to predict that in forty days it would be wiped off the face of the earth—a job comparable to condemning communism in the streets of Cuba. Any catechist assigned to spread the Good News to a class that has the reputation of being bad news should have no trouble identifying with Jonah.

Jonah does not take the time to go through a process of discernment or to consult his spiritual director. He does the natural, cowardly thing. He runs away. Jonah is so terrified that simply refusing to cooperate is not enough. He boards a ship bound for the faraway city of Tarshish.

Jonah's goodness, however, redeems him. First of all, as the Bible points out, he pays the fare on the escape ship. He is not a stowaway. Further, he honestly and humbly, if not prudently, admits to the crew that he is fleeing from his God.

All goes well for the runaway prophet until a raging storm attacks the ship. So violent is this storm that the sailors toss the cargo overboard to lighten the ship. Somehow, in the midst of keeping the ship afloat, the crew finds time to cast lots to see who is to blame for the weather. Of course, the lots accuse Jonah. Unaware that the Lord is closing in on him, our hero lies fast asleep in the hold. Quite a feat considering the thunder, the waves, and his conscience; but it is characteristically human.

Once prodded awake and apprised of the situation, Jonah suggests that the sailors dump him overboard to save themselves and the ship. They take his advice, and what follows is a conversion worthy of the *Guinness Book of World Records*. When the storm clears, all the sailors worship Jonah's God, the God who made the sea and the land.

Leaving Jonah in the sea for awhile, let us consider the manner of his shipboard witness. He does not preach a word to the sailors, but surrenders his life for their sakes. Through his self-sacrifice, the tough pagan sailors come to a knowledge of God. Ironically, when Jonah—a coward, a jinx, and an outcast—most looks and feels like a total failure, he succeeds.

Now for the only "fishy" part of the Jonah tale. While Jonah flounders in the swirling waters, seaweed clinging about his head, the Lord sends a large fish to catch him. Notice that the fish's obedience to the Lord in the face of an unpleasant task exceeds that of Jonah. But who can surpass Jonah's trust in the Lord when he prays a prayer of thanksgiving—not an act of contrition—from the belly of this fish. Again, Jonah shows himself the perfect model for catechists.

Although in dire straits, half-drowned, and eaten by a sea monster (and what catechist has never been in a similar position?), Jonah is still full of living faith and praise for God. Living up to Jonah's confidence in him, the Lord delivers Jonah, via fish express, from ship to shore. There Jonah is spewed out safe and sound, though probably a bit shaken and seasick.

After his little game of hide-and-seek, Jonah is ready for Nineveh. His drenching has called him to his senses, and he realizes that the Lord's will for him might well be the least of many possible evils.

Once in Nineveh, after only a single day of prophesying doom, Jonah surely merits the prophet-of-the-year award. For everyone in the city, including the king, fasts and sits in sackcloth and ashes. Even the sheep and cattle fast and wear sackcloth in sympathy with their masters, making the fields of Nineveh a sight to behold.

What was Jonah's secret? He was not a prophet of many words or the book named for him would be longer than four chapters. According to the Bible, his words were not accompanied by spine-tingling miracles. And he certainly did not bombard the Ninevites through the media. Except in a passive way, the mass conversion of Nineveh was not Jonah's doing at all. It was God's. When Jonah finally let God use him, great things happened. Literally, he was an overnight success. God was able to work through Jonah to save an entire city. Jonah learns that being a witness is being a tool in the hands of God. God speaks and acts through people who turn over their lives to him.

The proper place for the story to end would be right here with God so moved by the people's repentance that he decides to cancel their punishment. God's prophet, Jonah, is covered in glory. But the foolish, unpredictable side of Jonah's human nature crops up and prolongs the tale.

Instead of being thrilled at Nineveh's overwhelmingly positive response to his message, Jonah is angry that God changed his mind about destroying the city. He had been rather looking forward to seeing a spectacular fire and brimstone demolition of his enemy. Therefore, Jonah breaks into a complaining speech in which he pretends that he fled before only because he knew that God was going to forgive the Ninevites.

Strangely, in the course of his tantrum, Jonah pays God a memorable compliment when he says, "I knew that you are a gracious and merciful God, slow to anger, rich in clemency, loath to punish." Jonah concludes by declaring that he is so angry, he wants to die. After his outburst, the disgruntled man parks himself on the outskirts of the town to see if God will comply with his wishes and consume Nineveh.

What happens next is a lesson for catechists as well as for Jonah. The divine teacher prepares a concrete learning experience for his thickheaded and hardhearted prophet. In one day a shady gourd plant springs up to protect Jonah from the hot sun. The following day a hungry worm chomps on the plant and kills it. Jonah gets just as angry about the plant as he did about Nineveh. With that, God draws the moral from the withered plant. Jonah is concerned about one gourd plant. Softening the lesson with gentle humor, God asks, "And should I not be concerned over Nineveh, the great city, in which there are more than a hundred and twenty thousand persons who cannot distinguish their right hand from their left, not to mention the many cattle?"

Jonah apparently is speechless, for the story abruptly ends with that question. No doubt, knowing the value of personal life stories in his work, Jonah repeated the story of Nineveh over and over during the remaining years of his ministry. Now almost three thousand years later, Jonah's tale, as a book of the Bible, is still influencing people's lives.

Although he is sometimes called the comic relief of the Bible, Jonah is undeniably a man of no small stature. Later another prophet (who could also sleep through storms at sea), compared Jonah's three-day imprisonment in the whale to his own confinement in a tomb. Ever since then Jonah has been a sign and witness of the Resurrection.

What more could we ask of the patron of catechists?

CHAPTER 27

Personalize Scripture

The Bible is not like a letter addressed to "Occupant" or a duplicated letter. It is meant to be a personal letter from God to us. God speaks through it about our immediate situations and our relationship with him. You've seen this if you have ever experienced shared homilies or Bible study sessions. It's amazing how each person sees a different meaning in a text and how different verses touch different hearts.

To make students more aware that God is talking to them directly in Scripture use the following activities:

In Ephesians 1:3–14, for personal pronouns substitute the names of students in your class. It will read like this: "Blessed be God the Father of our Lord Jesus Christ, who has blessed Margaret with all the spiritual blessings of heaven in Christ. Before the world was made, God chose Michael in Christ, to be holy and spotless, and to live through love in his presence…" (*Jerusalem Bible*)

For a deeper appreciation of God's personal love for them, have the students substitute their names for *you* in Isaiah 43:1–5.

Instead of substituting their names, the students could insert their names in Scripture passages: "If, Kathleen, you want to be a follower of mine, renounce yourself, take up your cross every day, Kathleen, and follow me. What gain is it, Kathleen, for you to have won the whole world and to have lost or ruined your very self?" (Luke 9:23–25).

Students can experience that Scripture is God's word to them by having them select personal verses in different ways:

- **Type up a sheet of Scripture verses** and let the students choose one that appeals to them for reflection.

- **Cut apart the sheet of Scripture verses.** Put the slips of paper in a box, a bag, or a valentine candy box and let the students draw out a passage.

- **Insert the verses on slips of paper inside balloons.** Inflate the balloons. Let the students choose a balloon, burst it, and read their message. Or write the verses on inflated balloons, deflate the balloons, and then let each student take one to inflate and read.

- **Put the verses inside plastic eggs.**

- **Curl the verses on slips of paper** using the edge of a scissor blade. Attach one end of each slip inside the outline of a tree, a heart, or flowers drawn on the board or a bulletin board. Let the student pluck a verse from the board.

- **Remove the fortunes in fortune cookies, using a safety pin and tweezers, and replace them with Scripture verses,** buy ready-made Scripture cookies at a religious goods store, or make your own Scripture fortune cookies. Here are two recipes:

RECIPE #1

¾ cup butter	3 eggs
2 cups sugar	1 cup sifted flour
1 tsp vanilla	

Mix together butter and sugar. Add vanilla. Beat in eggs. Add flour. Drop by teaspoon on greased and floured cookie sheets, allowing 2 inches between. Bake 15 minutes at 375°. While cookies are warm, set a folded slip of paper with a Scripture verse on each and fold cookies in half and pinch them together.

RECIPE #2

3 egg whites	1 tsp almond flavor
¾ cup sugar	⅓ cup oil
⅓ cup flour	

Preheat oven to 375°. Beat egg whites until frothy. Beat in sugar, flour, almond flavor, and oil. Drop by teaspoons on greased cookie sheet. Bake about 7 minutes or until edges are brown. Add Scripture verses as in Recipe #1.

- **Put the slips of paper inside Bugles snacks.**

- **Make five-petaled flowers out of light, colored paper.** Write a verse in the center of each flower with a pen (not felt-tipped) and fold the petals over the center. Fill a large bowl with water. Have the students choose a flower and place it on the water. The petals will open slowly to reveal the verse.

Tell the students that the readings for the liturgy on their birthday might contain a special gift from God for them. Suggest that they go to Mass that day and listen carefully to the readings. When you send a card congratulating a family on a newborn, you might include the readings for the day of birth.

Encourage the students to adopt a Scripture verse as a motto for their life, as bishops do.

Johnny Appleseed made Scripture personal for others. As he went about planting seeds for apple trees, he also planted the seed of God's word. When he stayed at a family's house, he would tear out a page from the Bible that he thought applied to them and leave it behind. Give notecards and write comments to students that incorporate Bible verses. These tidbits from Scripture sent to friends used to be called "a word of salvation." Encourage your students to send people meaningful Scripture verses, particularly at special times in their lives. Small "pass-it-on" cards with Scripture verses can be purchased at religious goods stores and slipped inside greeting cards and letters. Include Scripture in your own letters and notes to students.

Designate a bulletin board or a panel of chalkboard as a "graffiti wall." Invite the students to add Scripture verses that strike them throughout the year.

Speak about someone in the Bible whom you consider a friend. Invite the students to tell about one of their friends from Scripture.

To bring Scripture into your daily life, have the class compile a calendar with a short prayer from the Bible for each day of the month. Each student may choose a page (date) to plan and decorate.

Warn the students that words of Scripture especially meant for us will not be printed in red; nor will we hear a trumpet blast. Rather we will experience a stirring of our heart. Stirrings of the heart need solitude and stillness to hear. Prayer is a gift; we can't hear it or evaluate it ourselves. But we can dispose ourselves to receiving that gift.

Scripture itself enlightens us on how God speaks through the story of Elijah the prophet (1 Kings 19:11–13). Elijah was instructed, "Go outside and stand on the mountain before the Lord; the Lord will be passing by. A strong wind was shaking the mountains, but the Lord was not in the wind. After the wind there was an earthquake, but the Lord was not in the earthquake. After this there was fire, but the Lord was not in the fire. Then there was a tiny whispering sound. Elijah hid his face in his cloak and went and stood at the entrance of the cave. The Lord spoke to him."

CHAPTER 28

Delve into Symbols

Delving into a verse breaks open God's word. Have the students ponder each word or phrase in a Scripture verse, considering its everyday meaning, its meaning in the context of the passage, and its meaning in their life. After each reflection, they might compose a brief prayer flowing from the word. Present the following example:

A lamp to my feet is your word. (Psalm 119:105)

Lamp A lamp gives light and enables us to see. Because of lamps we can carry on our daily activities when it is dark at night or during a storm. A flick of a switch floods a room with light. Lamps on the sides of roads guide traffic in the dark; lights guide airplanes and ships. God, thank you for the gift of light. Always be my light and let me be a light for others.

Feet Usually we don't pay attention to our feet. What a service they perform for us. They take us wherever we wish to go. God, guide my feet to good places. Let them hurry to be of assistance to others and to do good.

Word A word expresses our thoughts and feelings. It lets us know what others are thinking and feeling. Because of Jesus, the Word, and Sacred Scripture we are able to know and love God. Lord, let me read and study your word in the Bible and communicate it to others. Let me use it to guide my journey through life.

Help your students to become knowledgeable about symbols used in the Bible, for instance, water. We pray in Psalm 42: "As the deer longs for the running waters, so my soul longs for you, O God. Athirst is my soul for God, the living God." How much more meaning these words have when we are aware of the significance of water in the Bible. The Israelites were nomads who traveled through the desert; water was precious to them.

The symbol of water is found in the Bible from beginning to end. In Genesis, the garden of Eden is watered by a river that split into four rivers. In Exodus, when the Israelites are wandering in the desert, Moses strikes a rock at God's direction, and water gushes forth. In the Gospel of John, Jesus exclaims, "Let anyone who thirsts come to me and drink" (John 7:37). In the Book of Revelation when the new heaven and new earth are described, the one who sits on the throne says, "To the thirsty I will give a gift from the spring of life-giving water" (Revelation 21:6). An angel shows the writer a river sparkling like crystal, flowing from the throne of God and of the Lamb. On either side of the river grows the tree of life.

Then there is the water of baptism. As Jesus tells Nicodemus: "No one can enter the kingdom of God without being born of water and Spirit" (John 3:5). Water plays a role in the wedding of Cana and in Jesus' meeting with the Samaritan woman. All of these references to water in the Bible can come into play and enrich our praying of Psalm 42, if we are aware of them.

We can trace and ponder the appearances of many other symbols in Scripture like rock, birds, bread, fire, and trees. The more we teach our students the Bible, the more they will perceive the nuances of the words and the more depth their prayer will have.

(See Illustration V in the Appendix for a worksheet that helps the students explore trees in Scripture.)

CHAPTER 29

Use Quotations and Stories

Incorporate quotations about the Bible into your lesson plan or have them displayed in the classroom. To illustrate a point and make it memorable, tell a story about Scripture.

QUOTATIONS

A person whose Bible is falling apart probably isn't.

You may be the only Bible that some people will ever read.

Ignorance of the Scriptures is ignorance of Christ. —*St. Jerome*

Scripture enables us to know the heart of God through the word of God.
—*St. Gregory the Great*

You can understand the Bible only on your knees. —*Maurice Zundel*

Most people are bothered by those passages in Scripture which they cannot understand; but as for me, I always notice that the passages in Scripture which trouble me most are those which I do understand. —*Mark Twain*

All Sacred Scripture is but one book, and that one book is Christ, because all divine Scripture speaks of Christ, and all divine Scripture is fulfilled in Christ.
—*Hugh of St. Victor*

It is especially the Gospels which sustain me during my hours of prayer, for in them I find what is necessary for me. I am constantly discovering in them new lights, hidden and mysterious meanings. —*St. Thérèse of Lisieux*

We have such a great God that a single of his words contains thousands of secrets. —*St. Teresa of Avila*

When people hear us speak God's word, they marvel at its beauty and power; when they see what little impact it has on our daily lives, they laugh and poke fun at what we say. —*Anonymous Second-Century Christian*

Such is the force and power of the word of God that it can serve the Church as her support and vigor and the children of the Church as strength for their faith, food for the soul, and as a pure and lasting font of spiritual life. —Catechism of the Catholic Church, *131*

Let Christ's word in all its richness dwell (find a home) in you. —*Colossians 3:16*

As a rocket fires off a spaceship outside the earth into space, so the word can propel us into God's endlessness. —*Wilfred Stinissen*

STORIES

» Karl Barth, the great twentieth-century Protestant theologian, wrote some eighty books about the word. When someone asked him to summarize his life's work, he responded, "Jesus loves me. This I know, for the Bible tells me so."

» Terry Anderson was held hostage in Lebanon for almost seven years. It was reported that he gave the Bible credit for helping him survive. He read it from cover to cover fifty times.

» A woman in Scotland was so poor that her neighbors helped support her. They thought it was a shame, though, because the woman's son had gone to America where he had become rich. One day the woman defended her son. She explained, "He writes me every week and sends me a little picture. See." She showed them her Bible. Between its pages were hundreds of U.S. bank notes which the woman had kept there.

» During a war one village was harboring a good man who was loved by all. When the village was invaded, the commander said to the mayor, "We know you are hiding a traitor. Give him over to us, or we will torment you and your people." The mayor met with the village council and came to no conclusion. He then searched the Scriptures with a priest all night long. They found the verse, "It is better that one man die to save the nation." As a result, the mayor handed over the innocent man who was tortured and put to death.

Years later a prophet came to the village and told the mayor, "That man you handed over to be killed was sent by God to be the savior of this country. How could you have done this?"

"But the priest and I looked at Scripture and did what it said," explained the mayor.

"That's where you made your mistake," said the prophet. "You looked at the Scriptures. You should have also looked into the man's eyes."

» After being married many years, a Jewish couple was finally blessed with a son. He was their great delight, until it was time for him to go to the synagogue and learn the word of God. Instead of going to the synagogue, the boy went to the woods where he swam in the lake and climbed trees. When he came home, the news had already spread. His parents were ashamed. They consulted experts to change the boy's attitudes and behavior, all in vain. After each session, the boy again found himself in the woods instead of the synagogue. His parents were greatly distressed.

Then one day a great rabbi came to the village. The parents brought their son to him and explained the situation. The rabbi bellowed, "Leave the boy with me and I will talk to him." The parents had second thoughts, but they left their son with the giant of a man.

The rabbi called to the boy, "Boy, come here." Trembling the boy approached him. The great rabbi picked him up and held him silently against his heart.

The next day the boy went to the synagogue to learn the word of God. After that he went to the woods. The boy grew up to become a great man who helped many people. He often said, "I first learned the word of God when the great rabbi held me silently against his heart."

CHAPTER 30

Study the Holy Land and Maps

The Holy Land is called the fifth gospel. Acquainting your students with the land where Jesus walked underlines the fact that he is real. Familiarizing them with the features of the Holy Land helps them to understand and visualize certain Bible stories. Having grown up within walking distance of Lake Erie, I always imagined that the Sea of Galilee was like my lake. When I went to Israel, I was surprised to discover that, unlike Lake Erie, from the shore of the Sea of Galilee you can see the other side!

Obtain pictures or books about the Holy Land and display them in your classroom. Show slides of the Holy Land or a video or DVD about it. Invite someone who has been to the Holy Land on a tour or pilgrimage to speak to your class about the experience and what he or she learned. Direct your students to a virtual tour of the Holy Land as at www.ffhl.org or www.mustardseed.net.

Transform your classroom into the Holy Land. Post directional signs (N, S, E, and W) on the walls. Label the room, or have students hold labels, for the Sea of Galilee, the Dead Sea, the Jordan River, the Mediterranean Sea, Galilee, Samaria, Judah, and key cities.

Purchase blackline masters of maps of the Holy Land (or make them yourself) and duplicate them for the students. Have them label the geographical features and color the maps. By certain cities they might draw symbols for events that occurred there. Have them trace the journeys of Abraham, the Israelites during the Exodus, Mary and Joseph, Jesus, and St. Paul. (See Illustration X in the Appendix for a map of the Holy Land.)

See "Resources" (page 95) for suppliers of charts.

Resources

Material to complement the teaching of Scripture is abundant. In addition to the items in this list you can find other and older resources at bookstores, especially Catholic or Christian ones, and at your school, parish, or public libraries. You might also borrow them from other teachers and from parents.

CATHOLIC BIBLE STUDY PROGRAMS

Acts of the Apostles and the *Gospel of Luke* are two Scripture study programs for children from grades three through six. (Simon Peter Press, P.O. Box 2187, Oldsmar, FL, 34677; info@simonpeterpress.com)

Six Weeks with the Bible for Teens (Loyola Press, 3441 No. Ashland Ave., Chicago, IL 60657; 800-621-1008)

Thompson, Katie. *The Liturgy of the Word with Children*: *A three-year program following the Lectionary* (Twenty-Third Publications, P.O. Box 6015, New London, CT 06320; 800-321-0411)

BIBLES

The American Bible Society offers a number of Scripture resources including inexpensive Bibles, booklets, and bookmarks, some free. (1865 Broadway, New York, NY 10023; 800-322-4253)

The *Catholic Youth Bible* and the *Catholic Family Bible* include many insets and pages of relevant information along with ways to pray and live Scripture. (St. Mary's Press, 702 Terrace Heights, Winona, MN 55987; 800-533-8095)

The Catholic Prayer Bible, Lectio Divina Edition helps in reading the Bible prayerfully as it applies the method of lectio divina to the passages. (Paulist Press, 997 Macarthur Blvd., Mahwah, NJ 07430; 800-218-1903)

Numerous publications for Bible education, such as *The Encyclopedia of Bible Games for Children's Ministry*; *Playful Songs and Bible Stories for Preschoolers*; *Pray, Play Bible*; and *Pray Play Bible 2* (Group Publishing, 1515 Cascade Ave., Loveland, CO 80538; 800-2447-1070)

Glavich, Mary Kathleen, S.N.D. *A Child's Bible, A Child's Book of Parables*, and *A Child's Book of Miracles*. Little books for young children (Loyola Press, 3441 No. Ashland Ave., Chicago, IL 60657; 800-621-1008)

The *Saint John's Bible* is seven volumes of the *New Revised Standard Version* handwritten and featuring hand-illuminated art created under the direction of calligrapher Donald Jackson. (Liturgical Press, P.O. Box 7500, Collegeville, MN 56321; 800-654-0476)

ACTIVITY BOOKS, SUNDAY SHEETS, DEVOTIONALS

Catholic Corner Puzzle Books for Years A, B, C and Catholic Corner Children's Bulletins for each Sunday (World Library Publications, 3708 River Road, Suite 400, Franklin Park, IL 60131; 800-566-6150)

MagnifiKid! A booklet of sixteen color pages for each Sunday and major feast days (MagnifiKid! P.O. Box 842, Yonkers, NY 10702; 866-273-5215)

Children's Worship Bulletins for each week, sets for younger and older children (Children's Worship Bulletins, P.O. Box 6360, Beaufort, SC 29903; 800-992-2144)

Living Faith Kids. Daily Catholic devotions based on the day's Scripture (Creative Communications for the Parish, 1564 Fencorp Drive, Fenton, MO 63026)

An action rhyme series of eight booklets for children (Twenty-Third Publications, P.O. Box 6015, New London, CT 06320; 800-321-0411)

Erickson, Jenny. *My Favorite* series. Four activity books on the Bible (Twenty-Third Publications)

Glavich, Mary Kathleen, SND. *The Bible: God's Great Love Story.* An activity book for grades 3 through 6 with reproducible pages (Paulist Press)

Vox Wezeman, Phyllis. *50 Interactive Bible Stories: For children ages 5 through 8* (Twenty-Third Publications)

BOOKS ABOUT THE BIBLE

Camille, Alice. *Animals of the Bible from A to Z.* (ACTA Publications, 4848 No. Clark St., Chicago, IL 60640)

Klein, Peter. *Scripture Source Book.* (Our Sunday Visitor, 200 Noll Plaza, Huntington, IN 46750; 800-348-2440)

Paprocki, Joe. *The Bible Blueprint: A Catholic's Guide to Understanding and Embracing God's Word.* (Loyola Press)

Schneider, Mary Valerie, SND. *10 Wise and Wonderful Stories for Children: Celebrating Holidays and Holy Days.* Scripture-based stories (Twenty-Third Publications)

Snyder, Bernadette McCarver. *150 Fun Facts Found in the Bible.* (Liguori Publications, One Liguori Dr., Liguori, MO 63057; 800-325-9521)

PLAYS

Glavich, Mary Kathleen, SND. *Gospel Theater for the Whole Community.* A collection of reproducible plays for ninety-two gospel stories (Twenty-Third Publications)

Old Testament Readers Theater and *New Testament Readers Theater.* Read-aloud Scriptures for young Christians (Twenty-Third Publications)

VIDEOS

The Gospel for Young People. Six videos for grades three through six (Franciscan Communications)

CD-ROMS

The Catholic Youth Bible: New Revised Standard Version. (St. Mary's Press, 702 Terrace Heights, Winona, MN 55987; 800-533-8095)

The Catholic Youth Bible Triple Challenge: A Digital Trivia Game (St. Mary's Press)

St. Mary's Press Old Testament Companion (St. Mary's Press)

Bible Blast. A family Bible study program based on Cook Communications Ministries *The Picture Bible.* Contains stories and quizzes (Bible Blast L.L.C. 4405 W. 88th St., Tulsa, OK 74132; 918-446-4844)

HeavenWord Children's Bible. Coloring pages, puzzles, quizzes, notes, and paintings for 140 stories (The United Methodist Publishing House; cokesbury.com; 800-672-1789)

Live the Bible iLumina Gold Parents and Teachers Edition Quizzes and Lessons. (Tyndale House Publishers)

Kids Point and Play Bible. Games and activities, multimedia presentation of stories (Baker Book House)

DVDS

Vision Video offers dozens of Bible stories for children, such as the Bedbug Bible Gang. See www.visionvideo.com. Other DVDs available are these:

A.D. (Ignatius Press)

Abraham (Ignatius Press)

Animated Classics series: Daniel, David and Goliath, The Good Samaritan, He Is Risen, King Is Born, Miracles of Jesus, Prodigal Son, Ruth (Ignatius Press)

The Apostle Paul and the Earliest Churches (Ignatius Press)

Catholic Vision Bible Classics series (Oblate Media)

Footprints of God series: David and Solomon, Moses, Jesus, Mary, Over Holy Ground, The Gospel of John (Ignatius Press)

The Greatest Adventure series from Hanna-Barbera

The Greatest Story Ever Told

Peter, Paul (Ignatius Press)

Jesus Christ Superstar

Jesus for Kids (Ignatius Press)

Jesus Grows Up (Oblate Media)

Jesus of Nazareth (Ignatius Press, Oblate Media)

Jesus, What He Said, What He Did (Oblate Media)

Journey through the Holy Land

King of Kings (Ignatius Press)

Kingsley's Meadow: The Complete Collection (stories performed by kids) (American Bible Society)

The Last Supper (Ignatius Press)

Mary of Nazareth (Ignatius Press)

The Nativity Story (Ignatius Press)

One Night with the King (Esther) (Ignatius Press)

Paul of Tarsus (Ignatius Press)

Paul the Apostle (Ignatius Press)

Paul the Emissary (Ignatius Press)

Peter and Paul

Read and Learn Bible Interactive (American Bible Society)

St. Peter (Ignatius Press)

The Story of Ruth (Ignatius Press)

The Ten Commandments

The Twelve Apostles (Ignatius Press)

Walking the Bible (Ignatius Press)

Where Jesus Walked (Ignatius Press)

FELT FIGURES

More than 600 characters and objects for telling Bible stories (Betty Lukens, Inc., 711 Portal St., Cotati, CA 94931; 800-541-9279)

POSTERS, PICTURES, AND CHARTS

"The Holy Land," "Where Jesus Walked," "Paul's Journeys," "The Middle East Then and Now," "Genealogy of Jesus," and timelines (Rose Publishing, 445 Torrance Blvd. #259, Torrance, CA 90503; 800-532-4278)

Bible Poster Sets (4) (Concordia Publishing, 800-325-3040)

"Faith Charts: The Bible at a Glance." A six-page laminated card (Our Sunday Visitor)

Assorted material. (Creative Teaching, 54732 Shelby Road, Suite #231, Shelby Township, MI 48316; 586-992-2368)

MUSIC

Preschool through Intermediate:

Wee Sing Musical Bible (Tyndale Publishing)

Calling the Children (Oregon Catholic Press)

Rise Up and Sing (Oregon Catholic Press)

Kid's Praise Bible Songs (Maranatha! Music)

Hi God! Series (Oregon Catholic Press)

Stories and Songs of Jesus and *More Stories and Songs of Jesus* (Oregon Catholic Press)

Junior/Senior High:

Songs by Christian singers favored by the students

Top 25 Praise Songs. A yearly edition (Maranatha! Music)

SCRIPTURE-BASED HANDWRITING CURRICULUM

A Reason for Writing. Workbooks for kindergarten through grade six (Concerned Communications, P.O. Box 1000, Siloam Springs, AR 72761, 800-447-4332)

APPENDIX OF
ACTIVITIES AND ILLUSTRATIONS

BIBLE BOOK WORD SEARCH

Name: _____   Total Found: _____

The names of all the books in the Bible are hidden in the square below. They are horizontal, vertical, or diagonal. When you find one, circle it and cross it off the list. Books with the same name appear only once.

Matthew
Mark
Luke
John
Epistles
Acts of the Apostles
Romans
Corinthians
Galatians
Ephesians
Philippians
Colossians
Thessalonians
Timothy
Titus
Philemon
Hebrews
James
Peter
Jude
Revelation
Zephaniah
Haggai
Zechariah
Malachi
Genesis
Exodus
Leviticus
Numbers
Deuteronomy

```
L O X B E L T U J P H I L E M O N M R C O I V
G A L A T I A N S E S T R P X I L E T O B I T
N U M B E R S O C M R I D H S O T V X L N O C
B A J E E K N Q L U K E S E R E D S I O B I F
O C H H N V I A X N O E M S P A L O T S H T S
P T T U A T S E C C L E S I A S T E S S Y E G
L S V T M P A O G C I H K A A Z H Q T I M S E
E O J X I Y P T I E J O B N M H E Z R A X I R
V F U L R M R N I Y N S V S I O S X J N E N O
I T D S U J O E L O G E C D P G S W I S D O M
T H I F T R V T B Z N A S L N R A N V L M X A
I E T T H N E C H O C S I I X D L J E K M B N
C A H C U O R H E Y I A K P S T O I M X A T S
U P R A L S B I X O G Z E P H A N I A H T L D
S O N G O F S O N G S B U I K A I H S C T Q I
N S I R E V E L A T I O N O D J A R A X H I Z
E T I S Q X A H Z D E U T E R O N O M Y E P E
H L P M A R K Y A S T H F L A H S N U F W Y C
E E C O R I N T H I A N S M Z N S T E N I X H
M S B V O A A P H I L I P P P A N S L H J C A
I K X R U I Y H D O X Q U R A C X J C I U T R
A C U H E T M A S I R A C H O W A A U R D N I
H E S I F W B R Y P E Z E K I E L H A D G U A
J O N A H O S H A B A K K U K A L B I T E P H
J A D M A C C A B E E S G X M O Q A K E S O L
```

Joshua	Nehemiah	Proverbs	Lamentations	Obadiah
Judges	Tobit	Ecclesiastes	Baruch	Jonah
Ruth	Judith	Song of Songs	Ezekiel	Micah
Samuel	Esther	Wisdom	Daniel	Nahum
Kings	Maccabees	Sirach	Hosea	Habakkuk
Chronicles	Job	Isaiah	Joel	
Ezra	Psalms	Jeremiah	Amos	

ANSWERS TO
BIBLE BOOK WORD SEARCH

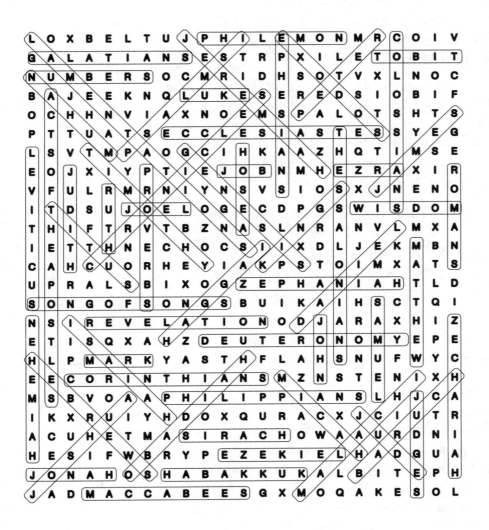

ISRAEL'S GREATEST KING
(1 SAMUEL 16–18, 26)

Not living up to his God-given call
Was the Israelites' first king, a man named _____. *Saul*
So Samuel looked for a new king for them
Among Jesse's eight sons, town of _____. *Bethlehem*
Who to anoint? Little thought Samuel gave it.
He chose the youngest, none other than _____. *David*

He was handsome and strong; the Lord's law he did keep.
The boy was called in from tending the _____. *sheep*
When King Saul grew moody and sorely depressed,
His friends told him David could cure him the best.
He could sing and compose; his mind was quite sharp.
So David soothed Saul with his songs on the _____. *harp*

"Let just one man fight me and if he should dieth,
You all lose," daily cried the giant _____. *Goliath*
For God's army, David accepted the dare.
Guarding sheep he had killed both a lion and a _____. *bear*

No other armor than God's help he got.
His weapon: five stones and his trusty _____. *slingshot*
In seconds the boy had Goliath quite dead:
Slung a stone to his forehead, then cut off his _____. *head*

David, a hero because of that deed,
Next was appointed Saul's army to _____. *lead*
His victories soon outdid Saul's former feats,
And people began to cheer him in the _____. *streets*
On hearing the shouts Saul with jealousy was filled,
Tried twice with his spear to have David _____. *killed*
David wandered the land with the king close behind
Until something one night changed angry Saul's _____. *mind*

As Saul lay asleep with his spear at his head,
David could easily have killed him instead.
But he warned his men not to attack,
Just stole the spear, and then quietly moved _____. *back*
The next morning Saul said, "You're more upright than I."
And decided to let all the hard feelings die.
Because toward God's leader David did the right thing.
He himself lived to become Israel's greatest _____. *king*

ILLUSTRATION C (page 15)

CHALK TALK FOR THE PRODIGAL SON

JONAH'S WHALE

Directions: Fold a square (8 1/2" x 8 1/2") of paper along the diagonal. Open the paper back up. Fold the left and right corners towards the middle so both sides meet. Cut along the center about 1/4 of the way for the tail. Take the top corner and fold it down 1". Then fold in half to "shut" both sides. Draw an eye on each side and spread the tail.

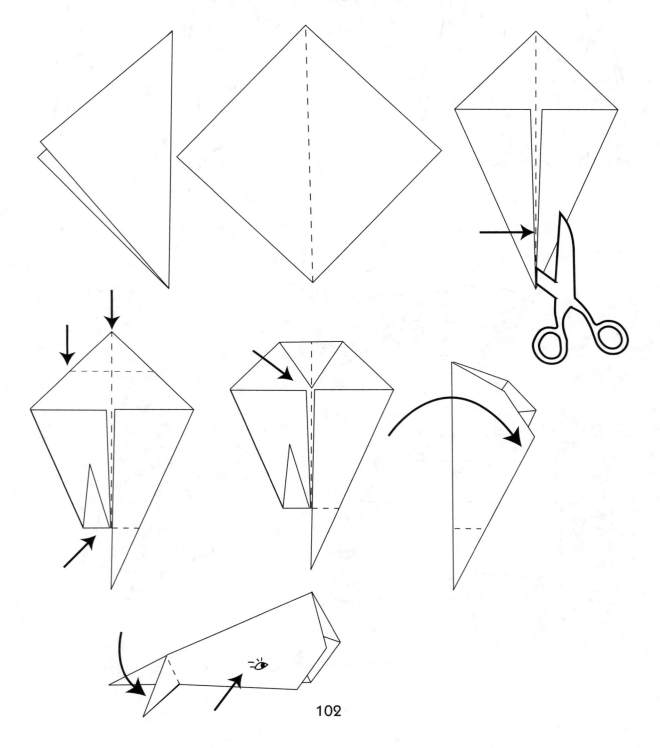

LOST SHEEP TRANSPARENCY

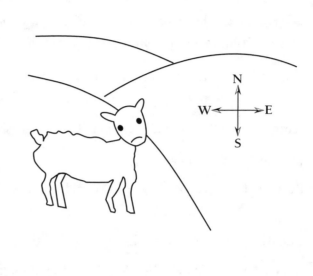

A PLAY ABOUT QUEEN ESTHER

Cast: Advisor, Ahasuerus, Esther, Haman, King, Maid, Mordecai, Narrator, Servant 1, Servant 2, Town Crier, Queen Vashti

SCENE ONE *The palace. Ahasuerus, Haman, and Advisor are dining. Servant 1 stands nearby. Queen Vashti is apart from them in her room.*

Narrator	King Ahasuerus held a great feast in Persia to show the wealth of his kingdom to his officials. All went well until the seventh day.
King	*(to Servant 1)* Go tell Queen Vashti to come here so everyone can see her beauty.

(Servant bows and leaves.)

Servant 1	*(to Vashti)* Your royal highness, his majesty commands you to appear before his guests.
Vashti	I don't feel like going. Tell the king I will not come.
Servant 1	*(bowing to king)* My Lord, the Queen will not come.

(Haman and advisor gasp.)

King	*(angrily)* How dare she refuse? What shall be done to punish her disobedience to a royal order?
Advisor	Queen Vashti has wronged you and the kingdom. When other women hear of this, they will imitate her. Issue a decree of divorce and find a more worthy queen.
King	Yes, I think I must.

(All exit.)

Town Crier	Hear ye, hear ye! The disobedient Vashti is no longer queen of Persia. Let all beautiful maidens be brought to the palace. The one who most pleases the king will become queen.

SCENE TWO *Two servants and Mordecai stand on the road.*

Narrator	Mordecai, a Jew, had adopted his cousin Esther, a lovely girl. Of all the women who came to the palace, Ahasuerus chose Esther to be queen. He did not know that she was Jewish. Then the king made Haman his highest official and ordered all to bow to him when he passed.

(Haman approaches.)

Servant 1   Here comes Haman. *(Servants bow.)*

Servant 2   *(to Mordecai)* Everyday when Haman comes by, you stand. Why do you disobey the king?

Mordecai   I bow to God alone. *(Exits.)*

Servant 1   *(to Haman)* My Lord, there is a man who refuses to bow to you.

Haman   What! Who is he?

Servant 2   The Jew, Mordecai.

Haman   I'll wipe those stiffnecked people off the face of the earth. *(Servants exit. Haman goes to king.)* Your majesty, in your kingdom there is a people who do not obey your laws. Issue a decree to destroy them, and I'll add ten thousand pieces to the treasury.

King   Keep your money, but here is my official seal. Do what you want.

(They exit.)

Town Crier   Hear ye, hear ye! The king decrees: Haman, second only to me and who I look upon as a father, has warned me. In his wisdom and loyalty, he has brought to my attention a wicked people living in our kingdom. We hereby order all Jews put to death by the sword on the fourteenth day of the last month.

SCENE THREE   *Esther's room. Esther is attended by Servant 2. Mordecai is outside the palace.*

Servant 2   Your highness, Mordecai is in sackcloth and ashes and he's crying loudly.

Esther   Go find out why.

Servant 2   *(to Mordecai)* The queen bids me ask why you are mourning.

Mordecai   Doesn't she know that Haman had the king order all the Jewish people killed? Tell her this and instruct her to plead with the king to save us.

Servant 2   *(to Esther)* Mordecai says Haman got the king to decree that all Jews be killed. He says you must speak to the king on behalf of your people.

Esther   Anyone who goes to the king without being summoned is killed on the spot unless the king extends his scepter. Tell him that.

Servant 2   *(to Mordecai)* Esther reminds you of the death penalty for those who go to the king without being sent for.

Mordecai	Tell her that since she's Jewish, she will be killed with the rest of us. Maybe she became queen just to meet this crisis.
Servant 2	*(to Esther)* Mordecai says you must go or be killed, too.
Esther	So be it. Tell Mordecai to have the Jews fast with me for three days. Then I will go to the king. *(Servant exits. Esther prays.)* Esther: My Lord help me. Put words into my mouth to save us from the wicked. Deliver me from my fear.

SCENE FOUR *The palace. The king is on the throne. Servant 1 is present. Esther and her maid are at the doorway.*

Narrator	After three days of penance, Esther approached the king. She was beautiful, but had to lean on a maid for support. The king looked up angrily. Esther grew faint, and the king sprang from his throne.
King	*(extending his scepter to Esther)* What is it, Esther? Even if you wish half my kingdom, you will have it.
Esther	If it please your majesty, come tomorrow with Haman to a banquet I shall prepare.
King	*(to Servant 1)* Have Haman fulfill Esther's wish. *(Servant bows and exits.)*
Esther	Thank you, my Lord.

SCENE FIVE *King's inner court the next day.*

Narrator	Haman's joy at the invitation was spoiled because Mordecai still refused to bow to him. His wife and friends suggested that he erect a gallows seventy-five feet high and ask the king to have Mordecai hanged. That night the king couldn't sleep. He asked that the record of events be read to him. In the course of the reading, the king realized that once when Mordecai had saved his life, he had never been rewarded. The next morning Haman sought to ask the king for Mordecai's death.
King	Ah, Haman. What should be done for the man the king wishes to reward?
Haman	*(aside)* He must mean me. *(to king)* He should wear the king's robe and crown and ride the king's horse. The noblest officials should clothe him and then go before him in the public square crying out, "This is what is done for the man whom the king wishes to reward."
King	Hurry. You are my noblest official. Do this for the Jew, Mordecai.

Haman	*(shocked)* As you say, O King. *(Bows and exits.)*

SCENE SIX *Palace banquet. Ahasuerus, Esther, and Haman dine, attended by Servant 1.*

King	Whatever you ask, Queen Esther, shall be granted to you.
Esther	O King, I ask that my life and the lives of my people be spared. We have been condemned to death.
King	Who and where is this man who dared to do this?
Esther	Our enemy is this wicked Haman!

(King exits angrily to the garden. Haman goes to Esther.)

Haman	My Queen, please save me. The king is so angry he will kill me.

(King returns.)

King	Will he assault the queen in my own house?
Servant 1	Your majesty, at Haman's house is a gallows on which he planned to hang Mordecai.
King	Hang this man on it. *(Servant takes Haman away.)* Esther, I give you Haman's house.
Esther	I will give it to Mordecai, for he is my cousin who adopted me.
King	Then I will also give Mordecai my signet ring. You and he may write to all the provinces whatever you see fit concerning the Jews.
Narrator	Thus it came to pass that the following message was proclaimed.
Town Crier	Hear ye, hear ye! Many ambitious men in high places take advantage of their position to wrong innocent people. Haman was such a man. You will do well to ignore the letter sent by him. The Jews may follow their own law. Everyone may help them defend themselves on the fourteenth day of Adar. That day must be celebrated forever.

OUR FATHER, ABRAHAM

(A CHORAL READING)

Chorus	Yahweh spoke to Abraham.
Yahweh *(strong, deep)*	Leave your country and your father's house for the land I will show you. I will make you a great nation; I will bless you. All nations of the earth will be blessed in you.
Abram	I will go forth, Lord God, to a new land, to a great blessing.
Chorus	Abram came to Canaan, the land that was promised.
Yahweh	To your descendants I will give this land
Abram *(questioning)*	But, Lord, I have no children. I am old; my wife is old.
Yahweh	Come outside and look at the sky. Count the stars if you can. So shall your descendants be.
Chorus	Abram put his faith in the Lord. And Yahweh made a covenant with him.
Yahweh	Walk before me and be blameless. Your name shall be Abraham. You shall become the father of many nations.
Chorus *(echoing)*	The father of many nations.
Yahweh	Your descendants will be kings. I will make a covenant with them. I will give them Canaan, and I will be your God.
Chorus *(echoing)*	Yahweh will be your God.
Yahweh	Sarah will bear a son. You are to name him Isaac. I will make him into a great nation.
Chorus *(echoing)*	A great nation.
Chorus *(normal)*	Sarah bore Isaac, son of Abraham. Count the stars if you can. So shall your descendants be. Abraham, father of many nations. But first your faith must be tried.

Yahweh	Abraham, Abraham. Take your son, your only child Isaac, whom you love. Offer him on a mountain that I will point out to you.
Solo 1	How can there be descendants?
Solo 2	How can there be kings?
Solo 3	How can there be blessings?
Chorus	If Isaac is killed? But Abraham went to the mountain with Isaac.
Isaac *(high voice)*	Father, here are the fire and the wood. But where is the sheep for the offering?
Abraham *(slow, sad)*	My son, God will provide the sheep.
Chorus *(growing in momentum and intensity)*	Abraham built an altar and arranged the wood. He tied Isaac and laid him on the altar. He reached for the knife to kill his son.
Yahweh	*(loudly)* Abraham. *(gently)* Abraham. Do not harm your boy, I know how devoted you are to me. *(growing in power)* I will bless you and make your descendants as countless as the stars of the sky and the sands of the seashore. And in your descendants all the nations of the earth shall find blessing.
Chorus *(peacefully)*	Abraham offered a ram in place of Isaac. Isaac lived to be the father of princes. His descendants were as countless as the stars. And all the nations of the earth were blessed through Abraham, the father of believers.

CALLIGRAPHY MODEL SHEET

abcdefghijkl

mnopqrstuv

wxyz AABC

DEFGHIJ

KLMNNOP

QRSTTUV

WXYZ

ILLUSTRATION I (page 29)

GENESIS ACCORDING TO ROOM 21

Adam   Hey, Eve, isn't this a nice place to live?

Eve   Sure, is Adam. Whatcha say we have a little snack?

Adam   Sure. What's your choice? We can eat anything we want.

Eve   Except the apples on that tree over there.

Adam   Oh, yeah, I forgot. Too bad, they look pretty good.

Eve   They sure do. How about having just one? One couldn't hurt.

Adam   Yeah, but Eve, the Maker said to leave that tree alone. Anyway, there's a lot of other things we can eat. Here, eat this peach. It looks juicy and sweet.

Eve   Thanks a lot, Adam. *Slurp.* Hey, you're right—it is pretty good. Adam, look at that snake in the apple tree over there.

Adam   Get away, Eve. It might be poisonous.

Eve   Oh, get out, it's only a harmless little snake. Couldn't hurt a fly.

Adam   Maybe not a fly, but it can hurt you. Now get away.

Snake   Don't be afraid. She's right. I couldn't hurt a fly.

Eve   Adam, are you playing some kind of joke on me?

Adam   Joke, are you kidding? This is no joke.

Snake   Hey, guys, so I talk. What's the big deal? I just came to tell you how great the apples are. Why don't you try one?

Adam   Because the Maker told us not to.

Eve   And anyway there are other trees.

Snake   That's not the point. The point is why let God boss you around? You don't have to take that. Go ahead. Enjoy an apple.

Eve   Yeah, why not? *Crunch.* Yum. These apples are great. Have a bite, Adam?

Adam   Yeah, why not? *Slurp.* Hey, we better get some clothes on. Here, wear this.

Eve   Thanks. You know, Adam, we've been tricked.

Adam   I know.

God   This way to the exit!

STUDY GUIDE FOR THE
CONSTITUTION ON DIVINE REVELATION

PROLOGUE

1. Why did the Synod write this document? *(It wants the whole world to hear the summons to salvation, so that through hearing it may believe, through belief it may hope, through hope it may come to love.)*

DIVINE REVELATION ITSELF

2. What was God's will revealed to us? *(That people should have access to the Father, through Christ, the Word made flesh, in the Holy Spirit, and thus become sharers in the divine nature.)*; Who is the mediator and sum total of Revelation? *(Christ)*

3. What gives us evidence of God? *(Created realities)*; What promise did God reveal through the ages? *(The promise of redemption)*

4. What did Jesus reveal about God? *(The inner life of God; God was with us to deliver us from the darkness of sin and death, and to raise us up to eternal life.)*

5. Who perfects our faith and helps us understand Revelation? *(The Holy Spirit)*

6. How does Revelation aid reason? *(Things beyond reason can be known by all with ease, with firm certainty, and without the contamination of error.)*

THE TRANSLATION OF DIVINE REVELATION

7. Who handed on the Gospel? *(The apostles)*; Who are their successors? *(bishops)*; What is the mirror in which we see God? *(Tradition and the Scripture of both Testaments)*

8. What does the apostolic tradition comprise? *(Everything that serves to make the people of God live their lives in holiness and increase their faith)*; In what sense does Tradition make progress in the church? *(There is a growth in insight into the realities and words that are being passed on. The church advances toward the plenitude of divine truth.)*

9. Where is the word of God found? *(Scripture and Tradition)*

10. Who is entrusted with interpreting the word of God? *(The living teaching office of the church alone)*

SACRED SCRIPTURE: ITS DIVINE INSPIRATION AND ITS INTERPRETATION

11. Why are all biblical books sacred and canonical? *(Written under the inspiration of the Holy Spirit, they have God for their author.)*; What truth does Scripture teach? *(The truth which God wishes to see confided to it)*

12. What must the interpreters of Scripture do? *(Search out the meaning that the sacred writers had in mind)*; What must interpreting Scripture take into account? *(Literary forms, patterns of perception, speech and narrative that prevailed at the time of the sacred writers; the conventions that the people of this time followed in their dealing with one another; the Tradition of the entire Church)*

13. What can the word of God in the human languages be compared to? *(The word of the eternal Father become man)*

THE OLD TESTAMENT

14. Through what people did God first entrust his promises? *(Israel)*

15. Why are the Hebrew Scriptures valuable? *(They prophesy Christ, provide an understanding of God and his dealings with people, show authentic divine teaching, and are a treasury of prayer.)*

16 Where does the Old Testament find full meaning? *(The New Testament)*

THE NEW TESTAMENT

17. Why do the Gospels have a special place? *(They are our principal source for the life and teaching of the Incarnate Word, our Savior.)*

18. What was the purpose of the writers of the Gospels? *(That we might know the truth about what Jesus said and did.)*

19. What do the other New Testament books do? *(Firmly establish those matters that concern Christ, formulate more precisely his authentic teaching, preach the saving power of Christ's divine work, and foretell its glorious consummation)*

SACRED SCRIPTURE IN THE LIFE OF THE CHURCH

20. What should the preaching of the Church and the entire Christian religion be nourished and ruled by? *(Sacred Scripture)*

21. What does Scripture do for the People of God? *(Enlightens the mind, strengthens the will, and fires the hearts of people with the love of God)*

22. What is the relationship of Scripture to theology? *(It is its soul and, together with Tradition, its permanent foundation.)*

23. Who should read Scripture? *(Clerics, priests, and others who, as deacons or catechists, are officially engaged in the ministry of the word; all the Christian faithful, especially those who live the religious life)*; What should accompany the reading of Scripture? *(Prayer)*

24. What will increased veneration of the word of God bring about? *(A new impulse of spiritual life)*

JESSE TREE SYMBOLS

Apple with two bites out of it *(Adam and Eve)*

Ark, rainbow, dove carrying a branch *(Noah)*

Sword of sacrifice *(Abraham)*

Bundle of wood, lamb in a bush *(Isaac)*

Pitcher *(Rebecca)*

Ladder, well *(Jacob)*

Coat of many colors *(Joseph)*

Burning bush, tablets of the Law *(Moses)*

Lamb on the altar *(Levi)*

Sheaf of wheat *(Ruth)*

Harp, crown *(David)*

Temple *(Solomon)*

Sword *(Judith)*

Whale *(Jonah)*

Scroll *(Isaiah)*

Six-pointed star and chain *(Esther)*

Baptismal shell *(John the Baptizer)*

Carpenter's tools, staff *(St. Joseph)*

Lily, decorated M *(Mary)*

City of Bethlehem, star, rising sun, key of David

(See Illustration L)

ILLUSTRATION L (page 35)

JESSE TREE

DANCE MOVEMENTS TO THE OUR FATHER

(Circle Formation)

Our Father
(Hold hands and walk in a circle.)

Who art in heaven
(Raise hands.)

Hallowed be Thy name.
(Fold hands in prayer.)

Thy kingdom come
(Sweep right arm back.)

Thy will be done.
(Bow head and cross arms putting hands on shoulders.)

On earth
(Gesture down with left hand.)

As it is in heaven.
(Gesture up with right hand.)

Give us this day our daily bread
(Cup hand in front as for receiving Holy Communion.)

And forgive us our trespasses
(Kneel on right knee, strike breast, and bow head.)

As we forgive those who trespass against us.
(Join hands as you rise. Walk in a circle.)

And lead us not into temptation
(Turn out from circle and shield face.)

But deliver us from evil.
(Extend arms out in front.)

Amen.
(Fold hands. Bow head.)

KINEPOSIUM GROUP PLACEMENT CARDS

SECRETARY 1 — 1	2	3	4	5
	1 2 3 4 5	2 4 1 3 5	3 1 4 2 5	4 3 2 1 5
SECRETARY 2 — 6	7	8	9	10
	1 3 5 2 4	2 5 3 1 4	3 2 1 5 4	5 1 2 3 4
SECRETARY 3 — 11	12	13	14	15
	1 4 2 5 3	2 1 5 4 3	4 5 1 2 3	5 2 4 1 3
SECRETARY 4 — 16	17	18	19	20
	1 5 4 3 2	3 4 5 1 2	4 2 5 3 1	5 3 1 4 2
SECRETARY 5 — 21	22	23	24	25
	2 3 4 5 1	3 5 2 4 1	4 1 3 5 2	5 4 3 2 1

BIBLICAL POEMS

CONCRETE BIBLICAL POEMS are poems in which the words shape the message.

```
      WHOEVER
     WISHES TO
   BE MY FOLLOWER
  MUST DENY HIS VERY
  SELF, TAKE UP HIS
   CROSS EACH DAY
   AND FOLLOW IN
    MY STEPS.
    WHOEVER
    WOULD SAVE
    HIS LIFE
    WILL LOSE
    IT, AND WHO-
    EVER LOSES
    HIS LIFE
   FOR MY SAKE
    WILL SAVE
       IT
```
LUKE 9:23–24

```
    LOVE          LOVE
  LOVELOVEL  OVELOVEL
 OVELOVELOVELOVELOVE
 LOVELOVELOVEHATELO
 VELOVELOVELOVELOV
  ELOVELOVELOVEL
   OVELOVELOVEL
    OVELOVELO
     VELOVEL
      OVEL
       OV
        E
```
MATTHEW 5:43–48

CINQUAINS

Line 1:	1 word that names the topic
Line 2:	2 words that define or describe the topic
Line 3:	3 words that express action about the topic
Line 4:	4 words that express feeling about the topic
Line 5:	1 word that is a synonym for the topic

Example: Judith
Lovely, holy
Conquering the enemy
Courageous through her faith
Heroine.

118

DIAMANTES (diamond-shaped)

Line 1:   1 word that names the topic

Line 2:   2 words that describe the topic

Line 3:   3 participles (-ing or -ed words) that describe the topic

Line 4:   4 words, the first 2 refer to line 1, the second 2 to the last line

Line 5:   3 participles that describe the word in line 7

Line 6:   2 words that describe the word in line 7

Line 7:   1 word which is the opposite of the word in line 1

(Hint: Compose the first and last lines first)

Example: "Mary Magdalene"

Sinner

Town prostitute

Longing, selling, crying

She encounters divine love.

Learning, laughing, giving

Jesus' disciple

Saint

FREE VERSE is a poem that has no rhyme or definite rhythm.

RAP is popular, rapid, beat-driven rhymes such as the following **Abraham: A Rap.**

Abraham had a pretty good life,
living in Haran with Sarah, his wife.
Then God called him one special day—
said, "Pack up your things. Be on your way
to a new fine land that I will show.
I will bless you if you do go.
People will be glad because of you.
You'll be great before I'm through."
Because Abram followed God's command,
God promised him and his kin the land.

But Abram and Sarah were very old
and had no kids to inherit, we're told.
Still God told Abram that by and by
his descendants would be like the stars in the sky.
What's more God made him leap for joy
by promising him a baby boy.
After meeting God, Abram was never the same.
God even changed his and Sarah's name.
Now Abram is honored by all as
"father in faith," who answered God's call.

A SAMPLE MEDITATION
ZACCHAEUS (LUKE 19:1–10)

Still yourself. Put everything away. Relax. Close your eyes.

Quiet your mind. Empty it of all thoughts and concerns about what you are having for lunch today or what you will do after school. Concentrate on God. God is here now, loving you. God is going to communicate a message that has particular meaning for you.

READ

Luke 19:1–10

RECREATE

Consider Zacchaeus, the wealthy tax collector, a VIP. He is probably a pompous, bossy man. He is not well liked. People know he lines his pockets with money stolen from them. Although Zacchaeus is a bigshot, he is short. This is his handicap. Maybe it even makes him defensive and tough. But one day Zacchaeus has an encounter that changes his life.

At first he is only curious to see a popular preacher. After straining in vain to look over the shoulders of the taller members of the crowd, he runs ahead and climbs up a tree. How ridiculous: an official hiding in a tree because of his weakness. But from his perch, Zacchaeus can see. In fact he gets to see more than he planned to. As Jesus passes below, he glances up and searches out Zacchaeus among the leaves. Jesus reveals his secret. He knows other secrets, too. He doesn't scold Zacchaeus or laugh at him. Rather, he honors him. He invites him into further friendship with him. Out of all the people in the crowd, it is Zacchaeus Jesus singles out, and he handles him with gentleness. Zacchaeus scrambles down out of the tree, maybe with a hand from Jesus, and he gives the proper response. He is delighted. Now that Jesus will dine at his house, Zacchaeus feels six feet tall. He is thrilled that Jesus did not wait for an invitation, but presumed on his hospitality, trusted him.

The crowd mutters that Jesus has gone to a sinner's house. Zacchaeus does have a reputation. After dining with Jesus, Zacchaeus stands before his family and guests and admits his sin. Then he is really big. He promises the Lord to change, and he offers to make up in a fitting way: greed is his fault; his remedy will be generosity. Salvation comes to all who welcomed God that day. The crowd, too, would benefit from Zacchaeus' conversion.

REFLECT

Let us reflect on this story. Each of us, like Zacchaeus, has shortcomings, weaknesses. Some we can't help—like having a crooked nose or a funny voice. Some we are more responsible for—like being short-tempered or short-sighted. As long as we try to keep our eyes on Jesus, even to the point of acting like a clown, being up a tree and out on a limb, there is hope. But we must be honest with ourselves. We might not have a crowd to point out our faults. But probably we have someone who hints at the thing about us that makes us squirm.

Jesus dwells within us. He says, "I like you, no matter what." We didn't have to earn his love. He invites us to dine at Eucharist with him, every day if we wish. The strength of our friendship with Jesus is sufficient power to effect a change in us. He doesn't give up on us when we fail. He encourages us like a mother or father teaching a child to walk. We don't have to hide. He comes for sinners like us. We can be open and stand tall.

RESPOND

Let us respond to this reading. In the presence of Jesus, look at the way you are living. What is your handicap, your shortcoming? How can you repair it? Ask Jesus to help you. Thank him for his loving care that always seeks out the sinner. [Pause]

Let us respond now with the verse we say at the end of the sacrament of Reconciliation: Give thanks to the Lord for he is good… (His mercy endures forever.)

(It's always a good idea to bring students out of a meditation gradually, using a short vocal prayer as a transition.)

A SEDER MEAL

(Candles should be lit.)

Leader   Blessed are you, Lord God, King of the Universe. In love you have chosen us for your service and made us holy through your commandments. You have kept us safe and brought us to this holy season.

All   Amen.

Leader   Let us pour the first cup of wine. *(Raises the cup.)* Blessed are you, Lord God, for this fruit of the vine. Continue to show your love.

All   Praise to you, Lord God, Ruler of the World. *(Drink from the cups.)*

Leader   Let us now dip our herbs.

(All dip parsley or lettuce in salt water and put it on their plates.)

Leader   Let us pray.

All   Praised are you, Lord God, King of the Universe, Creator of the fruit of the earth.

(The greens are eaten.)

Leader   *(Breaks a piece of matzoh and lifts it.)* This is the poor bread that our ancestors ate in Egypt. Let anyone who is hungry celebrate Passover with us.

All   God showed his love for us; we wish to share love with others.

(The youngest persons present ask the following four questions.)

One   Why is this night different from all other nights? On this night we eat bread without yeast in it. Why this evening do we eat unleavened bread?

Leader   In their hurry to leave Egypt, our ancestors had no time to wait for bread to rise, so they made bread without yeast.

Two   On other nights we eat all types of vegetables. Why tonight do we eat bitter herbs?

Leader   The herbs remind us of the bitter times in Egypt when we were slaves.

Three   On all other nights we do not dip greens in salt water. Why on this night do we dip them?

Leader	We dip greens in salt water to remind us that when we cried, God heard us.
Four	Why on this night do we eat reclining?
Leader	In ancient days to recline at meals was the sign of a free person. We demonstrate our freedom by reclining.

THE PASSOVER STORY

Reader	A reading from the Book of Exodus. (*Reads Exodus 12:21–28.*)

(*One of the group points to the items on the Seder plate.*)

Student	What is the meaning of the lamb symbolized by the bone?
Leader	The night when every firstborn male in the land of Egypt was struck down, homes marked by the blood of the lamb were spared.
Student	What is the meaning of the matzoh?
Leader	It is the flat bread our ancestors ate in their hurry to leave Egypt.
Student	What is the meaning of the bitter herbs and charoses?
Leader	They remind us of our hard service and the mortar we had to make for the Egyptians when we were slaves.
All	It is our duty to praise and thank God since God brought us from slavery to freedom, from sorrow to joy, from darkness to light.
Leader	Praise, you servants of the Lord. Praised be the name of the Lord.
All	Blessed be the name of the Lord forever.
Leader	Blessed are you, Lord God, for the fruit of the vine.
All	Praise to you, Lord God, Ruler of the World. (*Drink from the cup.*)

(*Matzoh is broken and passed.*)

All	Praised are you, Lord God, King of the Universe who made us holy through the commandments and these bitter herbs. (*Eat some of the matzoh.*)

(*Each person receives the horseradish and charoses and places it between two pieces of matzoh.*)

Leader	Praised are you, Lord God, King of the Universe who made us holy by your commandments and these bitter herbs.

(*Eat the matzoh. Supper is served at this point.*)

GRACE AFTER MEALS

Leader   Praise to you, Lord God, King of the Universe who keeps the world with goodness, with grace, and with infinite mercy. Your mercy endures forever.

All   God, our Father, keep and protect us.

Leader   Our God, remember us as you remembered our ancestors so that we may find grace, mercy, life, and peace on this feast.

All   Amen. *(Drink from the cups.)*

Leader   May Elijah's spirit enter the hearts of all. May he inspire them to love you, and may he fill them with the desire to build a world with justice and freedom for all.

(The door is opened for Elijah and then closed.)

Leader   *(Raises the cup.)* May the Lord bless and keep us.

All   Amen.

Leader   May God's face shine on us.

All   Amen.

Leader   May the Lord grant us peace.

All   Amen.

Leader   Blessed are you, Lord God, for the fruit of the vine.

(Drink from the cups.)

BIBLE BONANZA

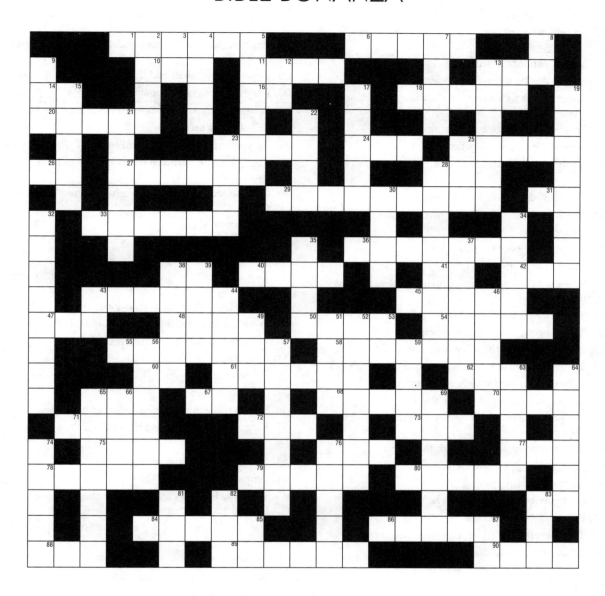

ACROSS

1. Song-prayers of King David
6. As punishment, Judah suffered the Babylonian ___
10. The God of Israel is ___ God
11. It gave Samson and Absalom problems
13. Nickname for the patriarch who doled out Egyptian food
14. Yahweh will be Israel's God ___ she does as he commands
16. To understand the Bible one must read ___
18. Reluctant prophet to Nineveh
20. Subject to Ezekiel's vision

DOWN

2. Jacob had twelve ___
3. ___ Israelite is a descendant of Israel (Jacob)
4. Jacob's first wife
5. An early holy shrine city
7. The kind of den Daniel was thrown into
8. Someone who shares the same faith as the Israelites
9. What Eve was made from
12. The ark and the Temple were ___ the holy city of Jerusalem
13. Angels went up and down ___ ladder

125

ACROSS continued

23. Ruth's husband, great-grandfather of David
24. God's dwelling on earth
25. Equal to man
26. Abbreviation for the book of the Law
27. Prophet who comforts through the idea of the suffering servant
28. Man of patience in suffering
29. Heroes during the Syrian persecution
31. Abbreviation for the part of the Bible containing Hebrew Writings
33. Prophet who anointed two kings
36. Isaac's wife (modern spelling)
38. Abbreviation for the first book
40. First murderer
41. What Solomon called Bathsheba
42. Number of tribes in the Northern Kingdom of Israel
43. Moses' sister
45. Mountain of God for Moses
47. Israel was ___ to make idols
48. Keeper of sycamores who violently attacked social injustice
50. Twin who gave away his birthright
54. Moses' priest-brother and spokesman
55. Book containing the story of creation
58. The father of believers, covenant-partner with God
60. Abbreviation for a very holy person
61. Great saving event of Jewish history
62. The priests here were killed by Saul for sheltering David
65. One uncomfortable quality of the desert
67. "The Lord ___ my shepherd"
68. Jacob's father-in-law
70. God's saving love is for the whole human ___
71. Helped Tobit and Jonah
72. The uncreated Spirit who created the universe
73. What Saul became due to pride and jealousy
75. Another name for prophet
76. Abraham's nephew
77. A delinquent priest-father that Samuel had to rebuke
78. A rainbow appeared ___ Noah's flood
79. City destroyed for its wickedness
80. The three men in the furnace prayed, "Cold and ___, bless the Lord"
83. What God answered when Job challenged him with a speech declaring his innocence
84. Southern kingdom named for the Messiah's tribe
86. Bread from heaven in the desert
88. God made the Reed Sea ___ for the Israelites
89. Solomon's greatest achievement
90. Abraham's descendants would be as numerous as the ___

DOWN continued

15. Number symbolizing purification
17. Almost sacrificed by his father
19. David's best friend
21. Prophet who attacked Baal and went up in a flaming chariot
22. Priest-scribe who founded Judaism by calling Israel back to the Law
23. Pagan God of Ahab and Jezebel
25. Prophet's prediction for sinful Israel
28. Prophet of the exile who was a suffering servant
30. Killed by his brother
32. Agreement between God and Israel
34. The ___ of the northern tribes to the southern tribes was ten to two
35. God guided his people through the desert as a pillar of ___
37. The Promised Land
38. Goliath was one
39. Revealed by God to Moses
43. Two letters that tell how Jonah found the earth after the flood
44. Israel's great liberator and lawgiver
46. What David didn't need to conquer Goliath
49. Biblical number of days for creation
51. First king of Israel
52. David's rebellious son
53. Abraham's hometown
56. Hebrew Queen of Persia who saved her people
57. King known for his wisdom and wealth
59. The first man
63. Famous tower of many languages
64. People who preserved the promise of a savior
65. What the Israelites interpreted as the means of God's direct intervention
66. His marriage symbolized Israel's relationship with Yahweh
69. David's prophet
74. King who sinned and repented
76. Describes Ruth
81. Abbreviation for the book about the lovely widow who cut off Holofernes' head
82. Amos called the wealthy ladies ___ cows
83. Originally occurred in Eden and resulted in the Fall
85. God predicted to Satan, "___ will strike at your head"
87. The judge Gideon fought with only 300 men ___ a sign of God's power

ANSWERS TO BIBLE BONANZA

```
        P S A L M S       E X I L E       M
R     O N E   H A I R       I     J O E
  F   N   A   I T     I     J O N A H   J
B O N E S   H   L E     N       C       O
  R   L     B O A Z   A R K   W O M A N   N
D   I S A I A H     R     A   J O B       A
  Y   J             A   M A C C A B E E S   O T   H
C   S A M U E L         B     R       R     A
O   H         F   R E B E C C A           A
V     G N   C A I N   L   M A       T E N
E   M I R I A M     R       S I N A I   I
N O T     A M O S   E S A U     A A R O N
A     G E N E S I S   A B R A H A M
N     S T   E X O D U S   D   N O B   J
T   H O T   I S   L A B A N   R A C E
  F I S H     G O D   L   M A D   B   W
D   S E E R     M   L O T   T     E L I
A F T E R     S O D O M   C H I L L   S
V   O R   J   F   N   Y     A       S H
I     J U D A H   A   M A N N A   I
D R Y   D   T E M P L E       S A N D
```

JONAH PICTURES

OVERHEAD PRESENTATION ON CREATION

THE WORD OF GOD
PRAYER SERVICE

OPENING SONG

Leader   Lord, we praise and thank you for the gift of your word. Through it we come to know your goodness and your love for us. Through it we find the way to happiness in this world and the next. Help us to respond to your word wholeheartedly.

PSALM 119 (ALTERNATE SIDES)

Side 1   My heart stands in awe at your word. (v. 161)

Side 2   Your word, O Lord, endures forever; it is firm as the heavens. (v. 89)

Side 1   I trust in your words. (v. 42)

Side 2   A lamp to my feet is your word, a light to my path. (v. 105)

Side 1   I will not forget your words. (v. 16)

Side 2   Of your kindness, O Lord, the earth is full (v. 64)

Side 1   My soul pines for your salvation; I hope in your word. (v. 81)

Side 2   Be good to your servant that I may live and keep your words. (v. 17)

READING *Matthew 7:24–27*

TIME FOR REFLECTION

Response: We praise you, Lord.

For your word that reveals you…

For your word that teaches us…

For your word that guides our lives…

For your word that speaks to our hearts…

For your word that lifts our minds to you…

For your word that assures us of your love…

Response: Make us open to your word, Lord.

That we may let your word touch our hearts…

That we may grow in understanding of your word…

That we may live by your word…

That we may bring others to know and love your word…

That we may appreciate your goodness in giving us your word…

CLOSING SONG

ILLUSTRATION V (page 85)

SYMBOLS IN SCRIPTURE: TREES

IN GENERAL

Draw a tree here.

- What is a tree?

- How is it different from other plants?

- What are trees used for?

FOR THE HEBREWS

- How did the Hebrews regard trees, especially after their desert experience?

IN YOUR LIFE

- How have you used trees?

- What tree has figured in you life—a favorite tree?

- What are some quotations, poems, and stories about trees?

- Why are we concerned about saving trees today?

IN SCRIPTURE

List Bible references to trees.

Now read Psalm 1:1–3, Matthew 13:31–32, Acts 10:39. Do they mean more to you?

INTRODUCING
PROCLAIMING SCRIPTURE

A fun way to teach proclaiming the word is to have individuals read a few verses exaggerating a fault. The class then tells what was wrong. Prepare slips of paper or cards, each with one of the directions below and pass them out to students. The following example is based on the passage John 10:22–25 in which the word "Jerusalem" occurs. The first card should be adjusted if another passage is chosen.

☐ Read the verses mispronouncing Jerusalem: Say "JAY roo SAIL um."

☐ Read the verses without looking up.

☐ Read the verses with no expression. Keep your voice flat.

☐ Read the verses slurring the words together.

☐ Read the verses stuttering and repeating.

☐ Sway back and forth as you read the verses.

☐ Read the verses too fast to be understood.

☐ Read the verses too softly to be heard.

ILLUSTRATION X (page 89)

MAP OF PALESTINE

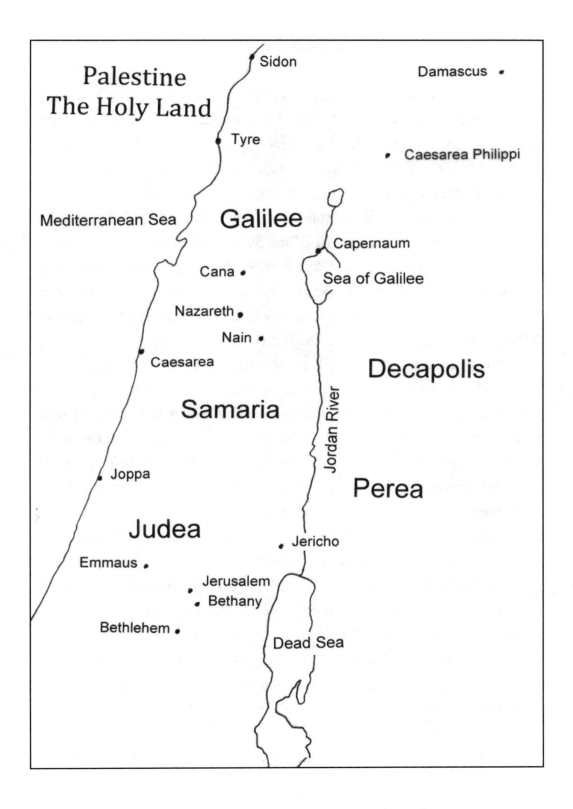

BIBLE BOOK HUNT

There are thirty books of the Bible in this paragraph. Can you find them?

This is a most remarkable puzzle. It was found by a gentleman in an air-plane seat pocket, on a flight from Los Angeles to Honolulu, keeping him occupied for hours. He enjoyed it so much, he passed it on to some friends. One friend from Illinois worked on this while fishing from his john boat. Another friend studied it while playing his banjo. Elaine Taylor, a columnist friend, was so intrigued by it she mentioned it in her weekly newspaper column. Another friend judges the job of solving this puzzle so involving, she brews a cup of tea to help her nerves. There will be some names that are really easy to spot. That's a fact. Some people, however, will soon find themselves in a jam, especially since the book names are not necessarily capitalized. Truthfully, from answers we get, we are forced to admit it usually takes a minister or a scholar to see some of them at the worst. Research has shown that something in our genes is responsible for the difficulty we have in seeing the books in this paragraph. During a recent fund raising event, which featured this puzzle, the Alpha Delta Phi lemonade booth set a new record. The local paper, *The Chronicle*, surveyed over 200 patrons who reported that this puzzle was one of the most dif-ficult they had ever seen. As Daniel Humana humbly puts it, "The books are all right here in plain view hidden from sight." Those able to find all of them will hear great lamentations from those who have to be shown. One revelation that may help is that books like Timothy and Samuel may occur without their numbers. Also, keep in mind, that punctuation and spaces in the middle are normal. A chipper attitude will help you compete really well against those who claim to know the answers. Remember, there is no need for a mad exodus; there really are thirty books of the Bible lurking somewhere in this paragraph waiting to be found. God Bless.

— *Source Unknown*

ANSWERS TO BIBLE BOOK HUNT

(Answers in order: Amos, Mark, Luke, John, Joel, Judges, Job, Hebrews, Esther, Acts, James, Ruth, Romans, Titus, Matthew, Genesis, Philemon, Chronicles, Daniel, Nahum, Hosea, Lamentations, Revelation, Timothy, Samuel, Numbers, Malachi, Peter, Exodus, Kings.)

This is **A MOSt** re**MARK**able puzzle. It was found by a gentleman in an airplane seat pocket, on a flight from Los Angeles to Honolu**LU, KE**eping him occupied for hours. He enjoyed it so much, he passed it on to some friends. One friend from Illinois worked on this while fishing from his **JOHN** boat. Another friend studied it while playing his ban**JO. EL**aine Taylor, a columnist friend, was so intrigued by it she mentioned it in her weekly newspaper column. Another friend **JUDGES** the **JOB** of solving this puzzle so involving, s**HE BREWS** a cup of tea to help her nerv**ES. THER**e will be some names that are really easy to spot. That's a f**ACT**. Some people, however, will soon find themselves in a **JAM, ES**pecially since the book names are not necessarily capitalized. **TRUTH**fully, f**ROM ANS**wers we get, we are forced to admi**T IT US**ually takes a minister or a scholar to see some of the**M AT THE W**orst. Research has shown that something in our **GENES IS** responsible for the difficulty we have in seeing the books in this paragraph. During a recent fund raising event, which featured this puzzle, the Alpha Delta **PHI LEMON**ade booth set a new record. The local paper, *The* **CHRONICLE,** Surveyed over two hundred patrons who reported that this puzzle was one of the most difficult they had ever seen. As **DANIEL** Huma**NA HUM**bly puts it, "The books are all right here in plain view hidden from sight." **THOSE** Able to find all of them will hear great **LAMENTATIONS** from those who have to be shown. One **REVELATION** that may help is that books like **TIMOTHY** and **SAMUEL** may occur without their **NUMBERS**. Also, keep in mind, that punctuation and spaces in the middle are nor**MAL. A CHI**pper attitude will help you com**PETE R**eally well against those who claim to know the answers. Remember, there is no need for a mad **EXODUS**; there really are thirty books of the Bible lur**KING** Somewhere in this paragraph waiting to be found. God Bless.

Other Books You Might Enjoy...

ALL GOD'S CHILDREN
42 Short and Joyful Stories for Children Ages 3 through 8
ANNE E. NEUBERGER

These delightful stories give children insight into the way other children live in far-off places like India, Turkey, and Iraq. Each offers guidelines for "before reading the story," and questions, activities, and prayers for "after reading the story."

104 pp • $14.95 • order 957972 • 978-1-58595-797-2

30 TEN-MINUTE PRAYER CELEBRATIONS FOR YOUNG CHILDREN
DEBBIE M. REPP

This exceptional resource taps into the hearts of little ones through simply-worded prayer celebrations. These are perfect for use with any topic and in any season, and each has a song, a brief Scripture passage, an "antiphonal" response, an activity that follows the theme, and a closing "thank you" prayer.

72 pp • $16.95 • order 957545 • 978-1-58595-754-5

37 CATHOLIC CLASSROOM CRAFTS
...in 20 minutes or less!
NICOLE T. WOODWARD

These crafts are the perfect complement to lessons on the bible, the church year, the gospels, and Jesus. The detailed directions and illustrations make each craft project easy for both catechists and those they teach. Also included is a companion CD that makes all components easy to print and distribute.

160 pp, with CD-ROM • $19.95 • order 957491 • 978-1-58595-749-1

50 INTERACTIVE BIBLE STORIES
...for Children ages 5-8
PHYLLIS VOS WEZEMAN

These delightful stories offer creative ways to review popular bible characters and events from both the old and new Testaments with young children. And, the author offers a variety of storytelling techniques, including action, echo, rhythm, and syllable stories—all involving children completely.

80 pp • 16.95 • order 957019 • 978-1-58595-701-9

GOSPEL THEATER FOR THE WHOLE COMMUNITY
MARY KATHLEEN GLAVICH, SND

Want to involve your whole parish community in "gospel theater"? Want to turn your faith formation gatherings into fun and interactive teachable moments? This invaluable resource will do both. Its ninety-two short and easy-to-stage gospel plays can be reproduced for all your parish catechetical gatherings.

160 pp • $29.95 • order 955639 • 978-1-58595-563-3

www.23rdpublications.com
1-800-321-0411